THE ART OF
SCRYING &
DOWSING

About the Author

Jenny Tyson (Nova Scotia, Canada) is an illustrator and writer, and practices and studies intuitive skills. She is married to Donald Tyson and enjoys working with different creative mediums.

THE ART OF
SCRYING & DOWSING

Foolproof Methods for ESP and Remote Viewing

JENNY TYSON

Llewellyn Publications • Woodbury, Minnesota

First Edition
Second Printing, 2022

Cover design by Shira Atakpu
Interior illustrations on pages 80, 82, and 87 by the Llewellyn Art Department. All other art
    by Jenny Tyson.

Llewellyn Publications is a registered trademark of Llewellyn Worldwide Ltd.

Library of Congress Cataloging-in-Publication Data

Names: Tyson, Jenny, author.
Title: The art of scrying & dowsing : foolproof methods for ESP and remote
    viewing / by Jenny Tyson.
Other titles: Art of scrying and dowsing
Description: First edition. | Woodbury, Minnesota : Llewellyn Worldwide,
    2021. | Includes bibliographical references and index. | Summary: "The
    author presents new, easy-to-use, and accurate techniques of scrying and
    dowsing that will help you find the answers you seek. It is particularly
    for those who are interested in scrying to see external locations,
    future events, hidden treasures, missing persons, or anything else you'd
    want to see using remote viewing"— Provided by publisher.
Identifiers: LCCN 2021017750 (print) | LCCN 2021017751 (ebook) | ISBN
    9780738767963 (paperback) | ISBN 9780738768120 (ebook)
Subjects: LCSH: Crystal gazing. | Dowsing.
Classification: LCC BF1335 .T97 2021 (print) | LCC BF1335 (ebook) | DDC
    133.3/22—dc23
LC record available at https://lccn.loc.gov/2021017750
LC ebook record available at https://lccn.loc.gov/2021017751

Llewellyn Worldwide Ltd. does not participate in, endorse, or have any authority or responsibility concerning private business transactions between our authors and the public.

All mail addressed to the author is forwarded but the publisher cannot, unless specifically instructed by the author, give out an address or phone number.

Any internet references contained in this work are current at publication time, but the publisher cannot guarantee that a specific location will continue to be maintained. Please refer to the publisher's website for links to authors' websites and other sources.

Llewellyn Publications
A Division of Llewellyn Worldwide Ltd.
2143 Wooddale Drive
Woodbury, MN 55125-2989
www.llewellyn.com

Printed in the United States of America

Other Books by Jenny Tyson

Spiritual Alchemy:
Scrying, Spirit Communication, and Alchemical Wisdom
(Llewellyn, 2016)

Upcoming Books by Jenny Tyson

The Art of Channeling:
An Original Method of Mediumship
(Llewellyn, 2022)

Contents

Figures

FOREWORD

What makes this book on scrying so special is its emphasis on the use of hidden targets. A hidden target is a target that you scry without consciously knowing what it is. Most forms of scrying involve seeking information about known targets. You might scry the Ark of the Covenant, for example, or Atlantis, or the assassination of Abraham Lincoln.

The trouble with scrying known targets is expectation bias. When you know what the target is, you naturally have presuppositions about its nature, its appearance, its circumstances, its function, and so on. These expectations in the conscious mind are much stronger and clearer than the information arising from the deeper mind during scrying. Expectations about the nature of the target tend to wash out and overwhelm the actual scrying information.

This reality of how the mind works presents a problem for the scryer. How do you scry the targets you want to scry without knowing what those targets are, thereby overwhelming the link to the deeper mind with expectation bias?

The method of scrying in this book presents a solution to this problem, which has hindered scryers down through the ages from obtaining accurate, factual information. That solution is to hide the target from the conscious mind while at the same time allowing the deeper mind to access it. In this way expectation bias can be avoided, enabling the clear but fragile link with the deeper mind to convey accurate, unbiased information to the conscious awareness.

The result is an extraordinary increase in the accuracy of the scryed information. Results may be achieved by relative beginners that exceed those of the great seers of the past, who struggled against expectation bias without ever understanding what it was or why it was a stumbling block. Even the greatest of them, such as Merlin, Nostradamus, and Edgar Cayce, had to combat their own expectations, desires, and fantasies to achieve unbiased, factual information, and all too often failed, because they were fighting against the natural processes of their own minds.

The scrying methods in this book liberate the seer from this inner conflict and allow the psychic fountain of the deeper mind to well up freely into consciousness, unhindered by expectations and doubts. These methods are based on almost a decade of intense study and practice by the author, Jenny Tyson, who has developed and refined them on a daily basis not only in her own work but also while teaching these scrying innovations to her students during classes and seminars.

These innovative techniques are based on the most modern practical research into the psychic abilities of the human mind, but have been streamlined and simplified by Jenny so that they are accessible to the average person wishing to learn to scry. She strongly believes that everyone has psychic abilities and can learn to scry accurately without needing to devote a large portion of their day to study and practice.

In no more than fifteen minutes, you can scry the secrets of the past and future, find things hidden beneath the sea and in the caverns of the earth, or soar far off through space to view other star systems and their alien inhabitants. Using these innovative, powerful techniques, you can scry more accurately than the greatest seers of history, who fought against their own expectation bias without realizing it. This book will liberate your mind to go anywhere in the universe and harvest the wisdom of the ages. This power was always yours, but you could not make use of it because your mind fought against itself. Free your mind and take advantage of its full psychic potential. The possibilities are truly limitless.

—Donald Tyson

INTRODUCTION
THE MODERN SCRYER

Scrying is the extrasensory perception of information at a distance through space and time. It encompasses both clairvoyance, which is extrasensory perception at a distance, and precognition, which is extrasensory perception of the future, but it is more than this. When you scry, you can also unlock the secrets of the past or gain knowledge about other dimensions of reality.

This book was written for those who have an interest in scrying, but not enough free time or energy in their hectic workday to develop their psychic abilities in traditional ways. It is a lightweight, minimalist system that focuses on efficiency, accuracy, and flexibility. It adapts traditional scrying concepts to a modern lifestyle by using short sessions and easy-to-learn techniques that have a high level of accuracy. Scrying and dowsing are traditional arts that have been reengineered and presented here using modern teaching and practicing techniques. Scrying and dowsing transcend time and space. They are aided by a special ritual, called the Lighthouse Ritual, that creates a quantum time loop for the purpose of guiding the practitioner to greater skill and accuracy.

Over the years of my involvement with the extrasensory abilities of the mind, I have frequently heard people say that they are not psychic, that they cannot scry. I decided to tackle this problem and discover how scrying works and how to break down the skills needed for scrying so that they can be taught easily and learned quickly by the majority of people who are interested in this art but have little free time. The result is an accessible system that can be used with good success by both working adults and busy students, a system that gives amazingly accurate results even without any training.

Scrying takes various forms. Traditional scrying involves inducing visions by gazing into a crystal ball, a mirror, a basin of water, or another polished surface, but you can also scry by casting various materials such as bones, shells, rice, or pebbles across a surface, and looking for aspects of images in the patterns that result. It is a very natural skill that does not require expensive tools or extensive, tedious training. It can be used for mundane purposes, such as the recovery of lost objects, but also to probe beyond the physical realm into the higher regions of Spirit. This art has always been the backbone of divination. Its flexibility allows it not only to predict future events but also to discover information about the past and present. Being able to perceive how spiritual energies manifest in the physical realm is helpful when trying to understand the world around us and in personal spiritual development. Being able to perceive spiritual beings is essential when working with angels and other nonphysical entities.

I first succeeded in learning scrying through a series of spirit communications that I related in my previous book, *Spiritual Alchemy* (Llewellyn, 2016). A spirit who identified himself as the famous Elizabethan alchemist and scryer Sir Edward Kelley taught me how to scry into a silver mirror that was tilted to reflect only the white ceiling of the room in which I worked. I recorded the colors and forms that appeared in the mirror as they changed before my eyes, and thus began a new era in my life.

The technique I learned from Kelley is not efficient and requires natural psychic ability to induce a vision. The traditional way to learn scrying basically involves staring at an object and trying to see images by focusing the mind and sight, coupled with physical stillness. It has changed little over the course of centuries. The majority of people who try this traditional method find it to be an exercise in frustration. I spent years modifying this technique and studying the responses of students to the various improvements I made, until finally I was able to develop the revolutionary new scrying method set forth in this book.

I found that utilizing principles from Joseph Buchanan's pioneering 1893 work *Manual of Psychometry*, coupled with aspects of Ingo Swann's remote viewing techniques, made learning to scry much easier. My goal was to devise a method that would enable the average person to scry both quickly and accurately. The system described in these pages is based primarily upon a combination of techniques communicated to me by spiritual entities, and inspiration received from the two sources I just mentioned. In addition, I used scrying itself to uncover the best techniques.

When the scrying method was tested, all of my students were able to learn it within half an hour and were able to use it immediately in fifteen-minute guided sessions. Everyone I taught it to had success in these experiments, even though none of those tested had any prior experience with divination or scrying. Two of my students had even considered themselves skeptics before learning the techniques, and were astonished at their own success.

All the items needed for scrying can be found in a typical household. Scrying without using any material tools of any kind is also taught for those situations that require the scryer to be completely discreet and to work unnoticed. My intention was to create a system that anyone could use even in less than ideal situations. I set the session length to fifteen minutes because this is long enough to achieve good results but brief enough not to interfere with ordinary daily activities. The technique can be practiced as little as once or twice a week yet still be successful, but I think that when you understand how well it works and how easy it is to do, you will want to use it more often.

This system of scrying is designed for everyone, regardless of their religious or spiritual beliefs. You do not need to be a Spiritualist or a Pagan or to have any particular belief system or training to use it successfully. Those from traditional religious backgrounds will find that it gives excellent results. It is not a belief system; it is a tool. And like all tools, what is done with it depends on the intention of the person using it.

I also include instructions on dowsing in this book. Dowsing is an ancient art that originally was used to locate veins of metallic ore, underground water, artifacts, buried treasure, and other items. I cover several different dowsing techniques. Traditional dowsing uses a pendulum, a bobber (a straight branch or a thin, flexible stick), or a Y-shaped willow branch. The dowsing I mainly focus on is a more modern system involving maps. I have used it successfully with treasure hunters and also in criminal investigations.

Dowsing is usually considered to be a have or have-not type of skill. That is to say, it is believed to be a natural ability that some people possess and others do not. I disagree with that premise. I have devised a dowsing system that is specifically designed for those who have difficulty working with pendulums and rod-type dowsing tools. It is called the dot matrix method. I found the inspiration for this method in dice divination used in Hoodoo circles, but I developed a way to do it so that it is under the control of the deeper mind.

I call the subconscious the *deeper mind* in my writings, because the term *subconscious* implies that it is not accessible to a person's awareness. This is far from the case. A thread can be opened from our consciousness to access deeper information, as well as spiritual power that lies underneath our everyday awareness. It requires a certain type of effort and an inner stillness to reach the deeper mind. Everyone has a deeper mind, and all human beings (and some nonhumans as well) have access to it.

Dowsing is simply a quick way to ask a question with only two possible outcomes. Anyone can ask the question, but it is up to the individual to learn to understand the answer. The dot matrix method of dowsing is an easy way to learn how to do this. It is a more objective method than pendulum or rod dowsing, and has the potential to be more accurate. I teach it in this book as the primary method to be used for the most accurate results. The dot matrix method is usable by everyone, can be practiced discreetly, and does not require specialized equipment. If desired, this original modern method may be supplemented by more traditional dowsing tools, such as a pendulum, a Y-rod, or a bobber.

I have included dowsing in this book because some of the questions you will want to know the answer to will have only two possible responses. This comes up quite a bit during scrying sessions. Dowsing is the easiest way to quickly work with these kinds of questions, and is readily incorporated into a scrying session. The unique method I teach can be used very discreetly when it is necessary to work in public settings with little time available.

In this book I address common problems with divination accuracy by introducing two new techniques. The first, which I call the grab bag technique, is a way to hide knowledge of what you are trying to scry from your own conscious mind prior to the session. This is done by placing a number of scrying targets into a bag on slips of paper, then drawing out a single slip without looking at it. In this way you select a target without knowing exactly which target you have selected.

This form of target obscuring allows you to cover the range of topics you are interested in, but hides the specific target or question you are working on. Randomizing targets so that the seer does not know what they are looking for during a session is standard practice in remote viewing circles. I have modified the remote viewing technique to allow greater focus. The original technique required more than a hundred targets to be put into the bag. Consequently, if you had a target of specific interest, it might not come up for months or even years. I have changed this to allow targets that are of interest to be done within a reasonable time period but without losing the accuracy that the grab bag method affords.

I have found that the grab bag method of randomizing targets (and the questions pertaining to those targets) greatly increases both the accuracy and the integrity of the scrying session. All the sessions that are used for case studies in this book were done with this target randomization system. The target was not known until after I finished the session. This can be intimidating to the beginner. However, if you follow the directions, it will become clear to you after a few attempts that the use of hidden targets is the best practice for scrying. In fact, I would encourage randomization by the grab bag method of target selection for any form of divination, including personal readings. Hidden targeting is being increasingly relied upon in various paranormal circles and is gaining popularity. The use of hidden targeting will eventually become the expected standard for divination.

The primary obstacle to accurate scrying is the practitioner's superficial, or conscious, mind. The superficial mind will impose beliefs and expectations that are based on spiritual, emotional, and mental past experience. These are called biases. The best way to eliminate them is to create conditions of scrying where the knowledge of the target is excluded during the session. If this knowledge cannot be eliminated, the scryer must be experienced enough to know what the biases feel like and what the session feels like when they are in contact with their deeper mind. Acquiring this level of experience requires practice with hidden targets.

For the majority of people, scrying should always be done with an obscured target. A hidden target is one from a target pool that you yourself created but that is unknown to you during the session, while a blind target is a target selected by someone else about which you have no knowledge of any kind. Both fall in the class of obscured targets. Blind targets are better than hidden targets, but if you are working alone, you will not be able to make use of them, since blind targets can only be selected by someone other than the scryer. Once you get used to scrying with obscured targets, you will shun prior knowledge of the target. Some practitioners actually get annoyed or even angry when someone "ruins" a session by talking about the target prior to the work.

The second original method I created to improve accuracy in scrying and dowsing is called the quantum time loop. Briefly stated, it enables the scryer to come into communication with their future self and, by so doing, acquire information about the target of the session that is revealed only in the future. This technique has been structured in the form of a ritual, which I call the Lighthouse Ritual. This ritual can also be used with traditional forms of divination such as the Tarot, runes, and geomancy. The original version of the ritual was inspired by my participation in a remote viewing group and involved the use of a spirit helper. The ritual improved my accuracy astronomically during testing. In the finished version presented in this book, the ritual does not require a spirit helper and is flexible enough to be used by anyone, even if they do not have any particular spiritual beliefs. It is a unique ritual that has proved to be invaluable in my own work.

The Lighthouse Ritual is easy to do. It does not require expensive equipment. Once the basic concepts are learned, it does not require any equipment at all. I teach the ritual using minimal equipment to start with in order to help the practitioner conceptualize the necessary components, but these tools may be dispensed with after the technique is acquired. This invaluable technique is explained fully in the final chapter.

The work going into this book was started even before my previous book, *Spiritual Alchemy*, was published. I wanted a system of scrying that anyone could use, that was easy to learn, efficient, and accurate. It is my hope that this book will enable you to explore the mysteries of the universe and grow in a personal way from your experiences. It brings an ancient skill into our busy, modern world. All of these techniques have been field-tested, and I am satisfied that they can be used safely, with reasonable ease and accuracy, by a beginner with no experience of any kind.

CHAPTER ONE
SCRYING TECHNIQUES

The method of scrying set forth in this book is different from the traditional methods you may be familiar with. In traditional scrying, scryers sit down before their speculums (scrying instruments) with the intention of scrying some specific time, place, or question. Or they sit down with a passive mind and allow images to arise without any control or forethought, taking them as they come as though they were watching a movie. That is to say, either they have a known, predetermined target in mind for their scrying or they have no target at all.

In the method of scrying presented here, we will use hidden targets. These are scrying targets that are not known to the scryer during the scrying session. Information concerning each target is written down on a slip of paper before the session begins. These slips are called *statements of intent* or *tasking statements*. At least four tasking statements for four different targets are prepared prior to a session. They are folded up so that their contents cannot be read without unfolding them, and placed together in what is called a grab bag. The use of the grab bag will be described in detail in the next chapter.

At the beginning of the session, the scryer selects at random one of these slips of paper, but does not read its contents. Instead, the tasking statement is set aside unopened, and the target is scryed without the conscious mind of the scryer knowing what the target is. Only after the session has been completed does the scryer open the paper containing the tasking statement and compare the information on the paper with what was scryed during the session.

The use of obscured targets is essential to accuracy in scrying. If the target is known before the scrying session begins, then the conscious mind will interfere with the ability of the deeper mind to scry and will introduce what is known as expectation bias—the scryer will see what they want to see, and this expectation will overwhelm the more subtle impressions of the deeper mind. Expectation bias is the bane of scrying, and the only way to avoid it is to hide the knowledge of the target during the scrying session. When obscured targets are used, scrying accuracy increases dramatically.

When the tasking statements are prepared by someone other than the scryer without the scryer's knowledge of what the possible subjects are, that is called being blind to the target. Working with blind targets is standard practice in remote viewing circles. I encourage scryers to make either a blind target or a hidden target their standard of practice. Hidden targets are usually used by a solitary practitioner, where they gather a collection of targets and randomly pick one so they do not know which target they are working on. This is not commonly done in remote viewing circles. Remote viewers prefer blind targets, which are collected and chosen by someone other than the viewer. Scryers can use either, depending on the situation. If you have someone who can collect and pick targets for you, then you can and should work with blind targets. A solitary practitioner can work alone making hidden targets, which are selected by the scryer but randomized and hidden for the scrying session.

The inherent limitation of a hidden target is the necessity for the scryer to select and prepare it prior to scrying. This means that there is some knowledge of the target in the memory of the scryer, even though the scryer does not know specifically which hidden target is drawn. The limitation of hidden targets can be overcome to some extent by building a large pool of targets ahead of the scrying session—for example, a hundred or more targets. Four of these can be chosen randomly without knowing their contents and placed in the grab bag. This works well for practice scrying, where the specific target can be anything.

The structure of the session will create the session focus and allow you to scry without interference from your beliefs and expectations. At the end of the scrying session, you will look at your tasking statement—the summary of the target information that is written in a single sentence on a folded slip of paper and placed in the grab bag, along with at least three other targets. You draw your target for the session at random from the bag without reading it and set it aside. When you look at the tasking statement after the scrying is done, in what is called the feedback session, and see how accurate your impressions were, it is like a miracle. It feels magical, like the heart of discovery itself. It is a bit intimidating to work with hidden targets at first, but the rush from the first few feedback sessions will forever eliminate the desire to scry unless you have obscured your target.

The following section explains the general pattern of a scrying session and how the targets for scrying are set up. Because we will be working with obscured targets, a structure must be put in place to help the scryer know what to focus on. This structure involves four categories of primary information. Following this structure will prevent a feeling of being lost and eliminate uncertainty about what to do next. It is an efficient procedure that will help the scrying go smoothly and improve its accuracy. Every step is important. For best results, the structure should be followed strictly and consistently.

Primary Information

Primary information may be defined as a broad concept or pattern perceived by the scryer at the beginning of the scrying session. It constitutes the first set of general impressions of the session, which are divided into four categories. Primary information is used to determine what you will be scrying during the rest of the session. The primary information provides the scryer with the focus needed to scry the target in an orderly and organized fashion. Using primary information gives a feeling of security and structure while at the same time allowing suppression of the biasing influences of the superficial mind. These biasing influences come from the scryer's life experiences, beliefs, and thoughts regarding the world around them and the target they are exploring. As much as possible, we must eliminate these influences from the session.

To determine what the primary information is, at the outset of the session you take a piece of paper and draw a square about four inches in width near the top of the page. This square represents a photo snapshot of the target site. You do not know which target you are doing at this time, but in your imagination this square represents the photograph of what you are supposed to scry.

Inside the square you make a small mark with your pencil or pen in three locations roughly equidistant from one another. I form these dots into a rough equilateral triangle that is contained within but covers as much of the square as possible. Let your intuition guide your hand when setting down these points. When you make each dot, think of it as a pinhole through the etheric veil. You are going to peep through these pinholes to look at the target. You are not physically doing this, but it is the mental picture I want you to have in mind when you put the dots in the square. You want to see as much of that picture as possible.

The square acts as a kind of photographic map of the target location, activities, and entities. The primary information is very basic information regarding your first impressions when you examine each of the three dots in the square. This allows you to make contact with your deeper mind and the target without creating a situation where you bias your scrying. You will examine each dot only with respect to the four primary information categories, called *aspects* or *points*.

When you look for primary information points, you will be choosing one of the four aspects for each of the three dots in the square at the top of your paper. Only these broad categories should be used. To use something more detailed will lead to biased scrying and loss of session integrity.

The four possible primary information aspects are as follows:

1. Object
2. Liquid
3. Presence (an intelligent, self-aware entity)
4. Activity/energy

Memorize this short list. It forms the backbone of the scrying session. It needs to be memorized so that it is reflexive and can be recalled instantly without thinking about it.

Each dot in the square represents at least one point of primary information that is present at the unknown target. You determine what aspect is at each point by touching the dot with the tip of your pencil or pen and immediately writing down one of the four possible choices from the list of *object*, *liquid*, *presence*, and *activity/energy*. Write this somewhere below the square on the sheet of paper. This work needs to be done as quickly as possible. Working too slowly will cause guessing and interference. This is what the action should be: touch a dot and write one of the choices. It has to be done as quickly as you can write. These points will become the focus of your scrying and take the place of the knowledge of the identification of the target.

Here are more detailed descriptions of the four primary information points.

Object

Objects can be natural or artificial. They can be land structures, buildings, artificial formations, or natural features. An object can be large or small. Spiritual objects also exist. Examples of things that are perceived as an object in the primary perception are houses, cars, archaeological artifacts, clothing, mountains, trees, sand, buildings, and monuments.

Liquid

Liquids can be large or small bodies of flowing, stationary, water-like, or heavy gaseous material. It is usually water, but it can be anything that moves in a fluid manner. It can be as large as the sea or as small as a glass of water. Sometimes gases will read as liquid. An example of this is the atmosphere of both Jupiter and Saturn. These read as a *liquid* aspect even though they are gaseous because they are so cold and dense. Most things that are not solid but move in a continuous flowing manner and have a state ranging from semisolid to heavy gas will read as *liquid*.

There is sometimes overlap between *liquid* and *activity/energy* or *object*. These overlaps are a normal occurrence and will not hinder the session. It is reflective of the nature of the universe. For example, humans are 60 percent water, yet we seem quite solid and do not have a visible continuous flowing quality, because that water is covered with a harder layer of skin. People also give the impression of *presence* and *activity*. These overlaps are not a reason for concern. Write the perception as it comes to you and use it for the scrying session.

Presence

A presence is an entity that is well developed enough to give a sense of intelligence, awareness, and activity. These can be human, animal, or extraterrestrial entities that are biological or spiritual in nature. Generally, the entity has to be fairly intelligent and well organized to read as *presence*. The interpretation can vary widely, however. Some scryers will read simpler creatures as a presence. It also depends on the context of the target and other factors like activity and energy. For example, a smaller entity such as a microscopic organism might read as a presence. This can be true especially if the focus of the tasking statement is to examine the life processes of that bacterium. If a small animal such as a mouse is moving rapidly in the target area while it is being scryed, then the animal might read as a presence because of its activity.

Presence is a very subtle perception, and like the overlap that occurs between *liquid* and *activity*, there is no cause for concern, as this overlap is reflective of the character of the universe. A perception of *presence* should be written down as it occurs and is scryed. Do not worry about complexity or strictness of the definition.

Activity/Energy

Activity and *energy* can be described as the emotional atmosphere or ambience of the location, event, or activity; the functioning of artificial objects; or the activity of living entities at the location. In spiritual and magical applications, it can be the interplay of different forces, be they elemental, astrological, or other types of spiritual currents.

Use of Primary Information Squares

As you progress through the scrying session, you may make more than one square if you wish to add more detailed data on the target. To start the session, use just one box. Three points of primary information should be identified per box. Other boxes may be drawn after you have finished describing the perceptions related to the first box. It is best to work one square at a time. Think of the square as a photograph of the subject of inquiry. You are defining broad, basic perceptions within that photographic snapshot.

Until you memorize the short list of primary perceptions, you should write them at the base of the square on your page before beginning. This way, you can work quickly without having to search your memory for the primary perceptions. Speed is important when doing this part of the session if your intuition is to function unobstructed.

To start your scrying session, you need three points of primary perception and one square. It will take you about fifteen minutes to fully scry the three points that form your initial perceptions. Additional points and squares can be used if you choose to do a longer or more detailed session. However, one square with three points should be adequate to give some basic information about the target, and will be about all you can handle within the fifteen-minute time parameter.

In summary of the method, the action you perform will be to draw a square about four inches in width and mentally associate it with the unknown target. Below the square, as a memory aid, write the list of four possible aspects of primary information: *object, liquid, presence,* and *activity/energy.* Quickly make three evenly spaced dots inside the square. Take your pen or pencil and set it on one of the points. Immediately write the aspect that you feel at that point. Write this somewhere below the square on the sheet of paper. Proceed to do all three points within the square, touching the pencil to a point and then without hesitation writing down the primary information aspect that you feel.

There is a possibility that you will sense more than one aspect of primary information at a point in the square. The best way to handle this is to write down both aspects and then scry them. This is a normal occurrence, and as you advance it may happen more frequently. When you find a primary aspect, you are taking a very small pinhole snapshot of the target. As you gain experience, you learn to perceive more through that pinhole.

The Scrying Session

Once you have gathered the three aspects of primary information, you can move on to scry. You scry each aspect in the order it was perceived until you have scryed all three points in the square. You work through one point of primary information at a time. So if your square has *object, liquid,* and *presence* as points of information, then you would choose "object" and scry for the aspects of the object, "liquid" and scry the perceptions related to the liquid, then "presence" and scry the visible aspects of presence.

The physical procedure is this: Each point of primary information is written again at the top of a new separate sheet of paper, and then they are scryed in detail one at a time. The impressions you receive about each aspect of primary information are listed below the aspect on its sheet. This constitutes the data of the session.

In this book I will cover several scrying techniques. These are actual scrying techniques, not just exercises. Each type of scrying will yield information about the target. You can use more than one type of scrying during a session. I have included several techniques in this book because everyone scrys differently. Some techniques will work better than others for a given student. All of these are traditional and ancient techniques, but I have modified them slightly so that they fit into a modern setting and can be used discreetly.

Scrying falls into three general categories: internal scrying, casting, and external scrying. I will describe each category in detail.

Internal Scrying

This is scrying using the imagination. There are no visual images outside of the mind in internal scrying. The imagination is employed in a structured way to provide visual information about the point of primary information. Internal scrying can be done with the eyes open and does not require an altered state of consciousness to perform. It is quick, and you need only a pencil or pen and a sheet of paper to do it. It works very well in settings that are not private, where stealth and a low profile are desired to prevent attention being drawn to you while you are working on a target.

Casting

Casting involves looking for aspects, lines, colors, and basic shapes that relate to the points of primary information in some way. In casting, you study the patterns in visually complex materials that you have mixed up in a random way, looking for relevant information. It does not require an altered state of mind, and is done with the eyes open. Casting materials can be rice, colored gravel, small bones, shells, or beads, to name a few. Casting can also be done with the Tarot if the cards have the right visual characteristics and bear abstract or surreal patterns and images, as the patterns on the cards take the place of the patterns of the cast material. I painted a deck of cards especially for casting. Tarot casting is one of my favorite methods of scrying.

Casting technique does require a little more practice than internal scrying. It can be used in a less than ideal public setting if the casting material is contained in a bowl or is of small size. Examples of such materials include a packet of colored rice or a deck of miniature Tarot cards.

External Scrying

External scrying is the quintessential type of scrying. This is where an actual vision is induced that contains information about the point of primary information you are exploring. The vision is induced internally, and basically externalizes what is generated through internal scrying. In this type of scrying, visual aspects are actually seen, or seem to be seen, with the eyes. Visions are fragmented and often dreamlike. They may be changing color patterns or simple shapes. Complex images are sometimes seen, depending on the scryer, but understand that you do not have to see dreamlike scenes in order to scry well. External scrying is not the same as dreaming or hallucinating. Most often it is a mental interpretation of the physiological artifacts that visually appear when you stare at an object for a length of time and induce eye fatigue. This physiological process is then programmed to provide information that you are looking for.

The appearance of external scrying will be different for each student. There are people who do have detailed dreamlike visions. However, there is no advantage to this dreamlike state other than it being an interesting experience. External scrying does require a slightly altered state of mind, but it does not require deep trance. You need to be focused and still, both physically and mentally, while you are working with this kind of scrying. Usually it is more a matter of knowing what to look for than of inducing a hallucination. Once you understand what it actually is that you are looking for, you will be able to do traditional scrying. This comes with practice.

The vision can be induced into what is called a speculum—a traditional scrying instrument such as a crystal ball, a mirror, a piece of rock crystal, a basin of water, and so on. It can also be done with closed eyes on the backs of the eyelids. The latter is the way I recommend if you need to be discreet, such as when you are in a public place and do not wish to be noticed.

External scrying requires the most practice. The skill lies not so much in acquiring the vision but in learning what to look for in the visual aberrations created by a prolonged fixed gaze.

Feedback Session

The feedback session is very important but is sometimes neglected. To start the feedback session after you finish your detailed scrying, you open the slip of paper containing your tasking statement to reveal the target. Then you take the information you obtained about the primary points when you did your scrying and compare it with the known information that is available about the target. Each point, and the aspects you scryed about it, is examined one at a time. For example, if you have a *liquid* aspect, you look at your target information to see if there is any form of liquid present. Then you look at the details of what you scryed for that aspect.

For example, let's say you scryed the color "blue" and the physical shapes "ribbonlike" and "narrow." You check to see if blue is present in any liquid at the target, if there is liquid moving in a ribbonlike fashion there, and so on. Each piece of information you obtained during the session needs to be examined. Sometimes, if you have photographs of the target, you may suspect that what you scryed is present at the target site even though it is not in the photos or other information. This should be written as a "maybe" beside that perception. Careful examination will help you improve over time. I write a check mark if the perception is present and a minus sign if it is not, and I circle the perception if it is likely to be there but is not seen in the photos I have of the target.

Feedback keeps your session grounded and helps to prevent fantasy in later sessions. What you do in a session will affect later sessions. This is why feedback is so important. The information you learn about your scrying session will influence sessions in the future. Neglect of feedback will result in a gradual deterioration of your skills.

Each detail in the scrying session should be examined and judged against the known information about the subject of inquiry. You must ask yourself, "Is this perception present at the target site?" If the answer is yes, then the perception is a hit. If it is not present at the location at that time, then the perception is a miss. The feedback session takes a bit of time to go through. If you are working a fifteen-minute session, you may only have enough time to date the session notes and the tasking slip. You can then compare information that you obtained while scrying with the known information about the object of inquiry when you have more time to do so.

CHAPTER TWO
TARGET SELECTION
AND PREPARATION

Next we will look at how to set up a scrying session. This includes target selection and creating tasking statements, which are also known as statements of intent. Correct setup will help you have the best possible success with your scrying. It is a part of the structure of this reengineered scrying system that is designed to improve the accuracy in this ancient art.

Choosing a Subject of Inquiry

First I will show you how to select targets. A subject of inquiry, or target, is a location, entity, or event that has activity and a visual or symbolic appearance. Ideally the target should have some concrete physical features that allow the scryer to do the feedback session mentioned in the previous chapter. It is important to do targets that have some verifiable features the majority of the time. Subjects of inquiry that do not have tangible features that can be compared to real-time information cause a destructive deterioration of scrying accuracy. For beginners, a high level of verifiable data needs to be present in the subject of inquiry. This is to facilitate the learning process. Sometimes these completely verifiable targets are called practice targets. Verifiable targets can also be precognition targets that are very black-and-white, such as stock market trends over a specific time period or the outcome of sporting events.

As you advance in skill, you can gradually increase the unknown aspects of your inquiries. For the intermediate to advanced scryer, there are usually photos and a brief description that can be used to compare the scrying data with the target. Encyclopedia entries are a good example of this type of inquiry. The more detailed entries are best for beginners. Experienced scryers can work with less detail in the subject description. I refer to the targets as *grounded* when they have a high level of verifiable information.

The second characteristic of a scrying target is that it should be hidden from the viewer. The solitary scryer will have at least partial knowledge of the target when the target is selected for the grab bag. This cannot be avoided since the scryer created the target pool. However, in the process of actually drawing the target for that particular session, the scryer will not know which of the targets in the grab bag they will be viewing. Because the scryer does not know at the time of the session which of the chosen subjects is being scryed, it is called a hidden target. This is the second characteristic of a good scrying target.

In the previous chapter, I discussed the use of the grab bag technique—the technique used to hide the subjects of inquiry for the solitary scryer. We will go over the specifics of this technique later in this chapter. It must be employed whenever possible, as it is essential to maintaining accurate scrying. Once you learn this material, you can set up a target in about five minutes.

There are three general types of inquiries in scrying: tangible, partially tangible, and esoteric. Let's examine each of them. These three describe the third characteristic of the scrying subject of inquiry.

Tangible Inquiries

A tangible target is one that can be verified in precise detail during the feedback session. You will have access to complete information about the subject of inquiry after you have finished scrying it, and will use this information to verify your hits and misses. Tangible targets help the scryer learn how to scry, and develop a sense of which methods of scrying work best for them. Targets with detailed known information are also the best targets for learning about yourself. It is important that you choose known targets to scry to help advance your spiritual development. The reason a known target helps with psycho-spiritual development is that it prevents you from going off into a fantasy while you are learning how to connect between your center of personal awareness and your deeper mind and Spirit. This enables transmission of true deeper knowledge and wisdom without the interference of the scryer's established beliefs, expectations, and fantasies.

Verifiable targets build confidence and skill. If you follow this guideline, you will learn how to scry with greater accuracy. When you use verifiable targets and establish a pattern of accurate scrying, then when the time comes to scry targets that are not verifiable, you will be able to do so with a more realistic understanding of the results. You will have a better understanding of how your hopes and fears, beliefs and thoughts, affect the perceptions coming from the deep Spirit. Also, when you read historical documents involving scrying, you will be able to better understand the perceptions of other seers, and even be able to correct, or add to, the information available.

Tangible targets are places, events, people, and activities about which a great deal of information is known. Photographs plus background information are usually available for these kinds of targets. Tangible targets are researchable and usually not controversial. Historically significant monuments, events, people, and places are often used as tangible targets. Historical targets provide interesting insights into the past.

A tangible target can also be a short-term prediction of the future. To qualify as a tangible target, the time span between the divination and the event predicted must be brief. An example of a precognitive tangible target is a ball game that will be played within a few weeks to a few months of the scrying session. Political elections are good targets as long as the prediction and the scrying session are done within a few weeks or months prior to the election. Any kind of stock or other market prediction that spans no more than a few months would be considered a tangible target.

A past historical event that has a substantial amount of information available about it would be a tangible target. An example of this is the Gettysburg Address delivered by President Abraham Lincoln in 1863, because many people were present to hear him speak and the event was widely covered by newspapers. It is not the date on which a past event occurred that defines it as a tangible target, but the amount of verifiable information available. That being said, targets in the distant past almost always have less reliable information available about them than do targets in the more recent past.

Tangible targets are the best type of target for a novice scryer. They are also useful to an experienced scryer for maintaining accuracy and detail in their work.

Partially Tangible Inquiries

The vast majority of targets that a scryer will work with are partially tangible inquiries. This is a target that has some characteristics and information that can be verified through documents and research or observed in a photograph, but there is a substantial level of information that cannot be examined in the feedback session. Partially tangible targets can be attempted once the practitioner has memorized the structure of the session and is able to work it smoothly and with accuracy. A good measure of accuracy for a beginner scryer is when you do a feedback session on a tangible target and find that at least half of the perceptions you obtained in your session were present at the target site. If this is the case consistently over a month, and you have the session structure memorized, you can move on to a partially tangible target.

The more potential for verification a partially tangible target has, the greater it benefits the accuracy of the scryer. Target information that is verifiable and can be judged in a feedback session has a strong positive effect on the scryer's accuracy. This effect is cumulative over time.

A partially tangible target will usually have a photo available but limited information. Good examples of this are planets and moons. We have photos of the planets in our solar system, such as Jupiter, but details such as the atmosphere of Jupiter and its surface are mostly unknown. At the time of this writing, none of the probes that have been sent to the giant planet have been able to penetrate very far into Jupiter's dense atmosphere. It is believed that the interior of the planet is a pressurized liquid, but this has never been documented. Jupiter would qualify as a partially tangible target, since we have photos and a good deal of information about the planet, but there are sizable holes in our knowledge.

Other examples of subjects that have a partially tangible characteristic are targets that will occur in the more distant future (in three months to three years) and puzzling anomalies of the past about which we have some information that is verifiable. Ancient monoliths and artifacts with characteristics that do not belong in their assessed time and place are examples of partially tangible inquiries. Ancient missing civilizations or unsolved mysteries such as alien abductions are partially tangible. Most paranormal phenomena that have more than one witness and some kind of media documentation would be considered partially tangible, as long as it is fairly certain that the documentation has not been fabricated.

These partially tangible inquires can be done by the intermediate to advanced scryer who has mastered basic tangible targets.

Esoteric Inquiries

Subjects that do not have a basis in physical reality, or are so advanced in technology that virtually no feedback is available on them, are called esoteric inquiries. If the target of the scrying session is completely esoteric, then there is always a risk of being misled or of drifting into fantasy. This can happen at any time and with any level of experience when scrying esoteric targets. Because of this, I recommend that while you are learning to scry, you do not use subjects of inquiry that are esoteric in nature. Until you establish accuracy in the art of scrying, the information sought should be tangible.

Once scrying skill and accuracy have been established through practice, the scryer can move on to working with conceptual, occult, or esoteric targets that have minimal to no verification potential. Examples of esoteric targets include exploration into spiritual domains such as spirit tables and sigils; concepts that involve physical aspects such as distant future information about locations and events; exoplanets, whose features cannot be verified; alien civilizations; spirit realms; and technologies communicated through spirit channeling or other spiritual techniques.

Atomic scrying, such as the scrying of the elements described in the book *Occult Chemistry* by Annie Besant and Charles W. Leadbeater, is mostly unverifiable. Theories like zero-point energy, and the mechanics and engineering of interdimensional travel, are mostly unverifiable. It is also possible that the verification available will be either controversial or intentionally hidden. These kinds of inquiries should wait until the scryer can work consistently and accurately.

The type of esoteric scrying where symbols and occult concepts are examined should be limited to 25 percent or less of the scryer's target list, even for an advanced scryer. The unverifiable aspects of this kind of scrying have a detrimental effect on the scryer's accuracy over time. To minimize this, it is a good idea even for an advanced scryer to maintain a list of more tangible targets to allow feedback sessions to be done.

The scryer can do consensus feedback for esoteric occult sessions. This means that the generally accepted meaning of a target that is viewed by multiple scryers is what constitutes the criteria against which the scrying session is examined.

I have personally been in situations where a group prediction was being made on a political election or a ball game. There were teams of four to eight people. In a couple of those predictions, I was the only person to make a particular prediction—the rest of the group made a different prediction. When the feedback was done, I was the only person correct in the prediction. I have also predicted the same outcome as the rest of the group and been wrong. So group consensus is not always accurate.

Characteristics of Good Scrying Targets

Subjects of inquiry must have certain characteristics in order to work well in a scrying session. This is particularly true for the beginner.

1. The target must have tangible aspects that can be used for the feedback session.
2. To maintain accuracy, the information about the target must be available to compare to the session data.
3. The target must be very specific.
4. The target should not contain intense emotional aspects if it is going to be worked solo until after the scryer has gained experience. A criminal investigation is an example of an emotionally intense target.

Creating the Grab Bag Pool of Targets

The practitioner should compile a list of at least four targets of interest for each scrying session. Once the topics are acquired, then the tasking statements need to be made. To start with, I would recommend four very different targets. Before the session, you will randomly pick one of that group out of the bag, set it aside, and scry it without looking to see what it is. The primary perceptions of the four targets should be as diverse as possible. For example, one target can contain water, another be focused on people, another be looking at an event, and so on.

The pool of targets needs to be at least four so that a significant level of doubt is created as to which target you are scrying. Having four targets in the grab bag is the absolute minimum number, even for an advanced scryer. If you find yourself trying to guess what the target is, then you need to increase the number of targets in the grab bag. Once you let go of trying to guess what you are supposed to be looking for, you will be able to reduce the number in the bag.

I initially had to start with about forty or fifty targets in the grab bag. I had to figure out how to create distinct targets in order to cut down on the number of possible inquiries in a session. I learned that if primary aspects of the targets were unique, then I did not need as many targets in the grab bag. I used to pick up a lot of Mars artifact targets, for example. I had to have about a hundred of them to minimize mental conflict involving guessing and labels. (Labels will be examined in the next chapter.) I found that if I mixed those Mars artifact targets with warm, tropical targets and activity or event-related targets, then I could go with fewer targets in the pool. If you use distinct targets, then you should not need more than ten or so in the grab bag.

You will need to keep the inquiry information about each target saved somewhere safe. I suggest bookmarking relevant web pages in a browser on your phone or other device. I have files that I keep with links to the information and photos that I use for feedback. I keep these as computer files. I may do more research when I do the scrying session feedback to try to validate or refute the information in the session accurately. This depends on the target.

The subject of inquiry is just a general statement of the topic I want to scry. The topic is broken down into specific questions that become the statements of intent. These are then put into the grab bag as tasking statements. After the session is completed, I compare the information scryed on the topic and the statement of intent used for the session with the known information available.

Statement of Intent

The statement of intent is the question you want answered about the target. You may have more than one question. To start with, pick the most interesting or important question to form your statement of intent. The statement of intent will tell your deeper mind what to look for. This is what actually goes into the grab bag, along with other tasking statements. The statement needs to have certain characteristics to be used effectively.

Specific Question

The inquiry needs to be specific. The statement of intent, or tasking statement, specifically describes what the scryer is looking for. The focus should be as narrow as possible. For example, if the scryer is looking at a monument such as the Great Sphinx of Egypt on a certain date in history, then everything needs to be spelled out and written down in the tasking statement. A good statement will have the exact location and time and specific information to be obtained.

The statement of intent should be specific to the following:

1. Time
2. Place
3. Entity
4. Activity

1. Time

The time needs to be as specific as possible. If you are doing a prediction, then a date when the event is supposed to occur must be the end date of the prediction. For example, if you do the scrying on August 5, 2019, and you want to predict the results of an election on November 3, 2020, then you need to specify the election date in the tasking statement.

If you are looking at an artifact and you want to explore when and how it was used but you do not know the exact date, then setting the tasking date is a little trickier. You can do this effectively by including information in the statement such as the following:

- When the object was built
- When the object experienced greatest use
- The period of time in history when the object can be best understood

2. Place

When you are working with a location, it needs to be a specific place. Generally it should be focused enough to be captured in three to four postcard-size photographs. This is a small area and applies mostly to tangible and partially tangible targets. An exception to this might be a planet that is relatively unknown. For example, the planet Jupiter is mapped with longitude and latitude. You could use this map of Jupiter to home in on a single section. If you were doing exoplanets, then very broad general descriptions would be obtained to start with, after which you would map the planet if you wanted more detail. All planets are spherical, more or less, so the mapping technique is to divide the sphere evenly and then number the degrees from the prime meridian, or zero degrees longitude line (in an exoplanet you would just pick this line arbitrarily); for the latitude, you start from the equator.

If you are doing a tangible target such as the Gettysburg Address, then the platform on which Abraham Lincoln spoke would be the location focus. You want to get as small an area as possible for your focus yet still cover the field of the information you are interested in.

3. Entity

I use the word *entity* because there may be people who want to try to target nonhumans in their scrying sessions. Angels and aliens comes to mind as examples. I have a strong interest in the UFO phenomenon and in alien matters, alien contact, ancient alien artifacts, etc. Your target may or may not be human. It should be focused on one or two individuals, if you find that your primary information or your pool contains a focus on individuals. Be sure to specify this in the tasking statement for the feedback session.

When you are doing entity scrying, there can be some ethical issues involved related to privacy. Just remember that what you can do to others can also be done to you. If you engage in spying on political leaders or celebrities, realize that they might have security or intelligence services that watch and prosecute should you publish such information. Everyone is vulnerable to having this done to them. You cannot protect yourself against it. It's pretty much a free-for-all when it comes to scrying. My advice is to avoid opening a door that you do not want opened on yourself.

It has also been noted that some alien species appear to have a natural defense in place that is unpleasant when encountered. As far as I know, the discomfort is only psychological. I do not know of anyone who has experienced physical retaliation. This is according to reports on the internet, which may or may not be reliable. I have had weird experiences doing this kind of target. It seemed to be either a psychological effect on my part or an expression of curiosity on theirs.

4. Activity

When you create your tasking statement, if there is an event or activity you want to focus on, then you need to be very specific about what that is. The mind is attracted to activity when you scry. You will always be drawn to where the action is by default. The challenge is to focus on the specific activity that pertains to your inquiry instead of leapfrogging to places of greatest activity and energy.

Your tasking statement is the key to that focus. Even though you do not see that statement during the scrying session, your deeper mind knows which target you drew. I believe this happens because the mind is naturally precognitive. It can see into the future to the time when you reveal your target to yourself after the session is completed. So your deeper mind works by knowing that information, plus focusing on what you wanted to look for.

The action in the statement of intent needs to be kept short and focused. Going back to the example of the Gettysburg Address as a subject of inquiry, each tasking statement could be a slightly different point in time, from the writing of the speech to the effect it had on the audience after it was delivered. President Lincoln's writing of the Gettysburg Address on the train needs to be a separate tasking statement from the delivery of the speech itself. The speech itself needs to be a different statement from the observation of the effect it had on the audience. The battle that occurred near Gettysburg prior to that day could be yet another target related to the same general topic and time period.

To provide feedback on the writing of the Gettysburg Address, I would do an internet search. I also have actually been to Gettysburg, Pennsylvania, so this would be a mildly familiar target for me. In my actual target pool I have a couple of replicated photos of the address, and I have watched documentaries about the speech. So I would only need to have my knowledge refreshed as I went through the scrying data and compared it to what is known about the actual event.

Imperatives

An effective tasking statement will have imperatives that tell you where to go and what to do. These statements need to be worded very specifically and concretely. The deeper mind tends to be extremely literal. It does not interpret information. When you give the deeper mind a tasking statement, it will go exactly to where you stated. It will not interpret your instruction at all.

Good tasking statements are short and direct. For example, if you are looking at an artifact, you might state, "Go to Iran at a date when this artifact was best understood and scry." The statement imperative should always contain the word *scry* or a similar term that expresses the action of seeing or discerning. The optional "Go to" statement tells where to open the channel. It is implied by the "scry" command, but it is useful to state it explicitly. The "scry" command tells you what to do once the channel is open. So these imperatives tell you where to go and what you want to do there.

Example of a Statement of Intent

The target you want to examine is the Great Sphinx, located on the Giza Plateau in Egypt. Here is a good example of a statement of intent for that target: "Scry and describe the exterior of the Great Sphinx and the activity around it on September 1, 2019, at 1500 hours."

At the time of this writing, this date is less than a week in the future. Once the date is past, I can verify the target using webcams, posted photos, and videos that are available online. This task is suitable for a beginner, as it contains information that is concrete and verifiable. The accuracy, or lack thereof, can be determined in a factual manner. The perceptions obtained in the scrying session either will be present at the target site at the time specified or will not be present. This statement of intent is time-specific, task-specific, and activity-specific. People may or may not be there and are not the focus of this target.

Tasking Must Be Objective

Task wording and intention need to be objective. What you believe will be the information obtained will not always match what is received in the session. Word your inquiry so you are not leading your deeper mind to tell you what you want to hear. If you are interested in the truth about the topic, be objective in the writing of the statement of intent.

Leading statements are an example of task wording that needs to be avoided. Going to our example of the Great Sphinx of Egypt, I would not say, "Scry and describe the mechanism behind the ear that opens the secret room of the Great Sphinx." I do not know if there is a room or a mechanism. If I suspect that there is and want to scry it, then I would have to word the statement more like this: "Describe any and all functions and objects related to the purpose of the Great Sphinx. Describe all hidden aspects of the Sphinx and their relationship to the known or suspected function and visual features of the monument." This is the proper way to state the inquiry task for this target.

The target now has a few verifiable components. The exterior of the Great Sphinx, the mechanical aspects, and most likely some of the hidden aspects should provide adequate verification for a moderately experienced scryer. These tangible characteristics can help determine the accuracy of the scrying session. Some of the photos may be fabricated or altered in some way. If this situation arises, you are likely to have random perceptions that do not make sense during the feedback session, or images related to the artist making the fabrication.

Written Statement of Intent

The inquiry needs to be written down. It needs to be associated with the file, bookmark, or folder where you have the known target information so that you can readily find and refer to the information file after the scrying session. The slips of paper used for the statements in the grab bag need to be identical in size and shape. So each statement of intent needs to be written in two places: it needs to be written on the slip of paper going into the grab bag, and it needs to be associated with the information that will be used for the feedback session after the scrying part is completed.

The Grab Bag

One of the most important aspects of a good scrying inquiry is that the target is hidden from the scryer at the time of the scrying session. The tasking statements that you have written down on identical slips of paper must be folded up so you cannot see any of the writing and in such a way that they all look identical.

Any bag or box that is large enough to put your hand into can be used as a grab bag. It should be of a size that is convenient to carry. Before you scry, take one of the slips of paper out of the bag. Without looking at the paper, put it in a safe place. Leave the rest of the slips in the grab bag. What is written on the slip of paper that you removed must remain hidden from you until you finish your scrying session.

After you finish scrying and recording your session, you will want to see what it is that you were supposed to be scrying. Remove the slip of paper from its safe location and make sure to date it with the time of the scrying session. The slip will have two dates: the date of the inquiry in the tasking statement and the date of the session when the inquiry was scryed. Also make sure to date the record of the information acquired during the scrying session. This way you will know which session goes with which inquiry. When you do multiple inquiries and sessions, it is easy to mix up the papers.

Dividing Topics into Questions

Another way of creating tasking statements is to divide the primary subject of inquiry into more specific tasks. Let us take one example and work with it: the construction and purpose of the Great Pyramid of Giza in Egypt.

Quite a lot is currently known about the Egyptian pyramids. We will be able to verify most of the information in the session through access to archaeological and museum information. We know approximately when the Egyptian pyramids were built, we know what they are made of, and we have some idea as to how they were made, the people involved in making them, and the Great Pyramid's location and size. I would divide the subject up into four tasking statements, like this:

1. "Scry and describe the construction process of the Great Pyramid, focusing on the architectural and engineering aspects."
2. "Scry and describe the original purpose of the Great Pyramid and how that purpose was carried out."
3. "Describe the origin of the concept of the Great Pyramid and why it was built."
4. "Describe any of the components of the Great Pyramid that are unknown or missing at the current time [specify time and date]."

There is one topic: the Great Pyramid of Giza. The individual tasks related to the topic are very specific and are different from each other. When subdividing a topic, it is important that the tasking statements be unique and have different visual aspects. For example, the "original purpose" has visual aspects of activity, energy/activity, and presence. The "origin" may focus on a presence and ambience. "Missing components" are objects. Any time a task is subdivided, the features need to be as distinct as possible so that you cannot guess what you are trying to scry. Guessing induces belief bias and should always be avoided.

By taking a general subject of inquiry about which we have an interest and subdividing it into specific statements of intent that are placed in the grab bag, we are able to take advantage of the method of hidden targets yet still focus the deeper mind on the information we wish to obtain. Scrying can be done without interference from the superficial mind and the bias it will employ to interpret the incoming perceptions.

I have taken the basic topic and made four specific questions related to it. When we do the scrying session, we will use only one of these questions. All four questions are written on pieces of paper, which are folded up and placed in the grab bag. It is of greatest importance that the scryer be unable to see any part of the question once the paper is folded. The paper must be folded in such a way that it will not come undone. The outward appearance of the folded papers should be identical. That means the papers must be the same type, color, and size, and folded the same way.

The papers are shuffled in the bag so they are mixed up. Take out one slip of paper. Do not look to see which question it is.

If you want to do all the questions, then you would do them in random order, without knowing which question you are working on. In that case, you would draw a slip of paper from the bag and write a number on the outside of it without looking inside to see what task is written on it. Once the numbers are written on the papers, put the slips in a secure place, such as a box or bag, and set them aside. If you only want to do one of the questions and do not have time to do all of them, that is fine—just grab one paper and place it in a secure location without looking at which question you drew. You will need to add to the grab bag to maintain at least four slips of paper in the bag for the next time you draw one out. You can use the same main topic of the Great Pyramid, or you can have a different topic in the same bag.

You are now prepared to start scrying. At first this method might seem intimidating, but it is the most effective way to avoid belief bias and fantasy. I have watched many psychics and have done quite a bit of work myself. It is always better when the subject of inquiry is hidden. Those who do not do so suffer the consequences of their actions. Their analytical labels and beliefs are presented to them in a showy and mentally pleasing fashion. They fall into fantasy and self-deception. I not only have watched others struggle but have spent a number of years myself working through this problem of belief bias. Hiding the subject is, as far as I can tell, the only viable and consistently dependable solution to it. This is a method that should be practiced at all times. It is not an exercise to prepare you for scrying. Scrying should always be done with the tasking questions obscured whenever possible.

This method works so well that you will eventually become annoyed if someone asks you to do a subject of inquiry and gives you any information about it before the session. Some of the better psychics will refuse to even do a session if they are given information on the subject prior to the session.

I used to be like that. I would not do a session if someone gave me information prior to doing it. I learned, however, that breaking up a subject into specific but unique questions and then randomizing the questions in the grab bag was effective at preventing scrying session pollution. The only requirement is that the subdivided questions be distinct in character.

Summary of the Steps to Create a Target

1. The target must have earthly, visible, tangible, and knowable aspects to it. This is called grounding.

2. The target must be obscured in order to limit belief and expectation biases.

3. To accomplish step 2, the subject is broken down into separate questions with distinct features. The questions are written on identical slips of paper, which are folded in an identical manner so the questions cannot be seen, and placed in a grab bag.

4. A slip of paper is drawn from the bag, numbered, and placed in a safe spot without looking to see which question it is.

5. The scrying session is done.

6. The paper is removed and the question examined. The paper and the written information of the scrying session are dated for future reference. If there is time, the known facts of the subject are examined against the information obtained though scrying.

Examples of Beginner-Level Targets and Tasking Statements

The following two targets are national parks and monuments. When you put the slips of paper in the grab bag, make sure that you put only the tasking statements in the bag (and not the target). If you add to this list, make sure that the information is mostly verifiable and that you have a very specific time tasked.

Target

Yellowstone National Park, Caldera Trail, August 8, 2019

Tasking Statements

1. "Describe the activity at the Yellowstone National Park Caldera Trail on August 8, 2019, at 3:00 p.m. local time."
2. "Describe the landscape and objects at the Yellowstone National Park Caldera Trail on August 8, 2019, at 3:00 p.m. local time."
3. "Describe any presence, human or animal, at the Yellowstone National Park Caldera Trail on August 8, 2019, at 3:00 p.m. local time."

Even though these tasking statements are in the same location (Yellowstone National Park), they are distinct in what they are asking for. In the first one, you are looking for activity. This is tasked so that it can be any activity. It does not just mean tourist activity. It could be caldera activity or animal activity. Even though there will not be any specific feedback available on the activity at Yellowstone National Park Caldera Trail for that exact day, you will have a general idea as to what is going on at that location on any given day in the summertime.

The second task is looking at the scenery. The scenery may show up in any of these sessions, but this is the focus of the task, so the data you obtain in the scrying session should reflect that tasking.

The third tasking statement is looking specifically for a sense of who is there on that day. The presence can include animals and humans.

These three tasks will go into the grab bag. Now let's take a couple other locations that are very different from Yellowstone National Park and add them to this collection.

Target

The Fortress of Louisbourg in Louisbourg, Nova Scotia, on August 13, 2019

Tasking Statements

1. "Describe the activity at the Fortress of Louisbourg on Cape Breton Island, Nova Scotia, on August 13, 2019, between 1:00 p.m. and 2:00 p.m. local time."

2. "Describe presence at the Fortress of Louisbourg on Cape Breton Island, Nova Scotia, on August 13, 2019, between 1:00 p.m. and 2:00 p.m. local time."

3. "Describe objects at the Fortress of Louisbourg on Cape Breton Island, Nova Scotia, on August 13, 2019, between 1:00 p.m. and 2:00 p.m. local time."

The Fortress of Louisbourg is on Cape Breton Island and is a historical monument complete with character actors, period food, and a reconstructed French village. It guards Louisbourg Harbour, which at the time the Europeans came to North America was an important port on the eastern shore of Nova Scotia. Summer is always busy and the activity never stops. The same parameters of presence, objects, and activity are used for the specific tasking statements. For feedback there is an abundance of information online, including videos, articles, and other media. The research regarding the specifics of the location can be done after the session. The subject of inquiry is a very general statement with minimal information. If you select one of these targets, then you can go and compare your data with information you find online and work through the feedback session doing detailed research.

Please be very clear about this: you do not put the target in the grab bag, but only the slips of paper containing the tasking statements. We now have six statements for the grab bag and two very different targets. This will greatly reduce any attempts to guess what is on the slip of paper when you draw it out of the bag.

CHAPTER THREE

INTERNAL SCRYING TECHNIQUE

There are two basic types of scrying: internal and external. Internal scrying uses imagination and psychometric "feeling." Psychometric feeling is when you sense something but you do not actually see it. You have the feel or experience of an object, presence, or energy without an actual visual image. Internal scrying occurs within the mind and deeper—beyond visual appearances, in the very heart of the seer. With internal scrying, you are not using external objects to induce a vision. It is like an experience in the imagination, the feeling you have when reading a story or daydreaming.

When doing external scrying, the seer is able to see visuals within a speculum, in the environment, or on closed eyelids. Also, the practitioner can use Tarot cards or a casting matrix, which is a mixture of rice and assorted small abstract objects such as bones and shells. The seer can observe patterns, colors, and shapes presented by the objects.

A speculum is a tool used for external scrying. Common speculums include such things as a crystal ball, a natural rock crystal, a mirror, and a pool of liquid such as ink, water, oil, or hot wax. Environmental scrying is done by gazing at a surface that has translucence and depth. This can be the sky, water, or the windows of a building. Environmental scrying can also involve discerning shapes, colors, and other information of objects in the environment. Aura scrying is an example of environmental scrying. The visual appearances that occur naturally or are induced by gazing provide the information the scryer seeks. Closed-eyelid scrying and environmental scrying are stealth methods that are very effective and useful in situations where no speculum or privacy is available to the scryer.

The type of scrying I will be teaching in this chapter is internal scrying. The internal method, if used properly, can be effective. It will sometimes be even more accurate than scrying using a speculum. When I teach scrying, I always start with internal scrying. This works best for those who do not have well-developed external scrying abilities.

Another advantage to the internal scrying method is that it increases accuracy when practicing traditional scrying. Visions scryed in a mirror, bowl of water, or other media originate from internal, deeper-mind sources. If you first learn to work from your mind and imagination, you connect with that same deep source. The external scryed vision is merely a projection of this internal imaginary process. Scrying in the speculum is inseparable from internal scrying with the imagination. However, for some people it takes training and practice to be able to project aspects of the internal vision onto an external screen, such as the crystal ball. The first step in that process is learning to use the internal vision.

There is value in the external vision, which is why I teach it and encourage seers to develop it. It helps us make spiritual connections to the deeper mind. It creates a visceral experience of the Spirit. I personally practice both types of scrying. The internal vision has to be finely developed in order to be fully and accurately utilized in a more traditional scrying session. The two are inseparable and work together for the desired result.

Setting Up the Scrying Session

In the first chapter I explained how to set up the session structure. When you start the scrying session, you need to be familiar with that structure to the point where you do not need memory aids to work with the primary information points of *object*, *liquid*, *presence*, and *activity/energy*. When you start a scrying session, you set up the session with the square at the top of the page, and three dots evenly spaced in the square, representing the pinholes through which you will perceive one or more of the aspects of primary information.

The scrying session is focused on those points of primary information. You examine the points when you scry. So the session should start with that procedure regardless of the type of scrying you do. Also, you use the grab bag containing at least four targets. The targets selected for this example of a short list are good ones for beginners. The shapes and colors are distinct and the objects are easy to scry.

For this first practice internal scrying session, let's pick four well-known monuments for the grab bag: the Eiffel Tower in Paris, the White House in Washington, DC, Notre-Dame Cathedral in Paris, and Windsor Castle in Berkshire, England. The general subject of inquiry for each one will be the same: "Go to _____ and scry the buildings and surroundings at 1600 hours on June 20, 2020." In all cases the time is local time.

The written tasking statements are as follows:

1. "Go to the Eiffel Tower in Paris, France, and scry the buildings and surroundings at 1600 hours on June 20, 2020."
2. "Go to the White House in Washington, DC, USA, and scry the buildings and surroundings at 1600 hours on June 20, 2020."
3. "Go to Notre-Dame Cathedral in Paris, France, and scry the buildings and surroundings at 1600 hours on June 20, 2020."
4. "Go to Windsor Castle in Berkshire, England, and scry the buildings and surroundings at 1600 hours on June 20, 2020."

These four tasking statements are written down on identical slips of paper, which are folded so that the writing is not visible, and placed in the grab bag. One of them is drawn out and set aside without looking at what is written on it.

June 20, 2020, is a Saturday. At the time I am writing this, it is in the future. When this book is published, it will be in the past. You can move anywhere in time and make your targets at different times if you want to compare how time affects the scrying data. For this session, however, the goal is to become familiar with internal scrying. I am assuming you have the list of the four aspects of primary information memorized. For the first session I am just going to do the primary information points without the scrying.

The White House Session:
Primary Information Aspects Only

The square is drawn at the top of your sheet of paper. I make three dots in a triangle pattern that fits in the square, with the dots regularly spaced to give me a good overview of the subject of inquiry. Touching the first point, I pick up *object*, and write that as my first perception. I then move to the next point, which is toward the bottom of the square, and pick up *liquid*. I go to the third point and perceive another *object*. So my three primary points for this target are *object*, *liquid*, and *object*. Because I am just working through the points of primary information, that is the end of this session. I now have to go to the feedback stage to compare my information with the target.

I reveal my tasking statement and it is number two, the White House. The statement of intent is "Go to the White House in Washington, DC, USA, and scry the buildings and surroundings at 1600 hours on June 20, 2020."

There are objects around the White House, so that is accurate, but I am not too sure about the liquid. The National Mall and the Lincoln Memorial Reflecting Pool are too far away and should not appear in the session data. So I check on a map of Washington, DC and find two large round fountains on the White House property. The fountains are large enough to register as a liquid. All three of my primary perceptions are present at that location, though I would say the liquid is not the best hit. For a beginner it would be considered a hit. For an advanced scryer I would call it off-focus but still a hit, since there is substantial size to the fountains. Generally when I perceive liquid, it is a more sizable body of water, unless the liquid is important to the primary task. This is one of the things you learn over time as you practice.

On your own, you should take several target groups like this and practice primary perceptions. When you are able to draw the square, set down the dots, and pick up the primary perceptions smoothly, you can move on to the next step.

The Real Nature of Scrying

Primary information points are like opening the door. The next step is scrying. There are specific things you need to focus on and look for when you are scrying. There are also things you need to avoid. This may be different from your expectations of what scrying is and how it looks. It is important to understand this. When scrying was first used as divination, movies were not in existence. The idea that scrying is like watching a movie is an error that arose from expectations in modern times. Scrying for most people appears only as flashes and fragments mixed in with ideas and imagination. It does not matter what type of scrying you do. If you are watching a movie while you scry, you are probably in a fantasy or sitting in front of a television screen.

There are a few gifted people who can mentally go to the target site and view it, and this also happens rarely to experienced but less gifted scryers. But being mentally projected to the target and visually seeing it is a rare occurrence. My goal is to teach those who do not have a great deal of natural talent how to scry accurately and consistently. Most of the time you will be experiencing what I describe as the "normal" scrying experience. There is no advantage to the full projection experience when it comes to accuracy. The scrying experience itself is not a factor in your hit/miss rate. Comparing Edward Kelley and Nostradamus, two very famous scryers, is a good way to understand this misconception of the "movie screen" scryer.

The prophet Nostradamus had the best descriptions of scrying I have seen in historical writing. He used a basin of water and stirred the water with a laurel wand. He was far more accurate in his work than Edward Kelley was when it came to real-time events and his perceptions of them. Nostradamus appears to have seen small bits and flashes. You can tell this by the way he wrote his quatrains. Each line of a quatrain is a scrying perception. It looks like he had four short sessions a night, and pieced a quatrain together based on those quick flashes and insights. I reached this conclusion by examining how the quatrains are put together and comparing it to my own experiences. If you look at those two things, it is not hard to figure out what was going on in his scrying sessions.

Edward Kelley used a crystal ball as his speculum for most of his work. He experienced a more movie-like vision when he scryed. However, he had poor accuracy when it came to predicting and describing physical events. His scrying was focused on obtaining the knowledge of alchemy by conversing with spirits who claimed to know how to perform the operations. Dr. Dee and Kelley wanted to understand how to transmute metals and gems—this is mineral alchemy. If you compare the information Kelley obtained to what his goal was, it is not hard to see that there was not much information scryed that was relevant to their primary focus, in spite of hundreds of pages of results from the movie-like visions he had in the crystals.

The esoteric system of Enochian magic that was developed from Kelley's scrying sessions is certainly interesting, and there are aspects of that system that are of value. I learned quite a bit from it about how scrying works and what to avoid. He was able to work with alphanumerics with some efficacy. It is possible that the Angelic language he transmitted is a nonhuman alien language. Its effectiveness in conjuring spirits and doing séances has been well documented. However, when you compare Kelley's scrying information to the focus of the sessions, which was the secret of alchemical transmutation, the quality of information was not very good in spite of the intensity of Kelley's visions in the speculum.

Regardless of the type of scrying you do, you need to understand your perceptions. This comes with practice. Do not focus on making that perception more movie-like or try to force it to fit your expectations of what scrying is or how it looks. By comparing Edward Kelley to Nostradamus, I am showing you that there is no advantage in accuracy to the stereotypical scrying vision as opposed to the scrying that perceives bits and pieces that have to be stitched together into a basic description. In fact, there may be certain advantages to the latter when it comes to accuracy.

Accuracy is the focus of my scrying techniques. The experience of movie-like vision scrying is interesting, but the novelty wears off. The advanced practitioner wants accuracy. I think that is what you want, too. We are not going for an unusual experience. The idea here is to teach you to scry dead on target with your natural ability.

Internal Scrying Procedure

When you do internal scrying, you sit with a sheet of paper in front of you, pen or pencil in hand. You can work with your eyes open. You are focusing internally, using your mind and imagination.

After the primary information points have been obtained, the next objective in the internal scrying method is to write and sketch your visual perceptions of these aspects. With scrying, the main focus is on the visual description of the inquiry. When you do this internally, you are using your imagination. The sensation is like feeling your way though the inquiry, and sometimes imaginary images will pop up in your mind. In internal scrying, these distinct visual images usually occur sporadically. The session may have a few images, many, or none at all. It is more of a sense of psychometry, which is psychic touch, and of feeling your way around.

It is almost like you put the target into a paper bag and feel the outside of the bag to describe what is in it. You cannot guess exactly what is in the bag, but you can describe aspects of it. Occasionally a pinhole develops in the bag, and you might see a color or texture. This is pretty much what internal scrying feels like when you first do it. This is not just an exercise—you can actually do this and perceive quite a bit of interesting and accurate information about a target. It is a real method of scrying. It is from this kind of perception that visions rise up both in the internal awareness and sometimes in vision. Internal scrying is both a means of obtaining information in its own right and a way to promote development of perception-based visionary abilities.

You will want to document your perceptions of the inquiry using descriptive terms and sketches. I will go over the process of sketching first.

Sketching is done by perceiving the primary information point you are focusing on, then drawing only the outline of that perception on your paper. It is best to try to sketch the outer edge of what appears in your imagination, and to do so as rapidly as possible. It does not have to look pretty, but it does need to be associated with the primary information point you are working with. Even though I am an artist, most of my scrying sketches will be stick figures and very general blobs and shapes. The session needs to progress quickly. Speed helps to prevent guessing and intellectual interference. It is undesirable to try to make sense of the sketches while you are drawing them, as this will tend to close down the deep-mind channel to the inquiry. Sketch the outline of the primary information and use arrows to indicate places of activity on the outline.

The second objective is to describe in words the primary information and the sketch you just drew. A descriptive word is usually an adjective, adverb, or verb. Adjectives modify or describe nouns, which are persons, places, and things. For example, in the phrase "a heavy hammer," the adjective "heavy" describes the noun "hammer." Adverbs do the same sort of thing for verbs, or action words. For example, in the sentence "He ran fast," the adverb "fast" describes the verb "ran." Verbs are action words, such as "jumps," "laughed," "drove," "walk," "remembered," "flew," and so on. Verbs are good for descriptions. However, nouns should be avoided, because they represent explicit things and visualizing them can lead to expectation bias.

For example, if you were describing a red mailbox on a post, you would not use the nouns "mailbox, box, mail, post, wood, metal, red." Those would create expectation bias. Instead, you would describe it with such words as "upright," "narrow," "capped," "painted," "oblong," "opens," "closes," "holds," "contains," "dented," "daily," and so on. You describe impressions that leave the mind open, not explicit things that close the mind with their finality. Labels are usually incorrect or misleading. As experience is gained, you will note that you occasionally guess correctly. But regardless of labeling accuracy, you still have to maintain the structure and break down all labels into descriptive components, or you will fall into a trap that will decrease your accuracy. It is a discipline that has to be maintained. This is one of the secrets to accurate scrying. The breakdown of labels is discussed later in this chapter.

Scrying emphasizes sight, but there can be impressions that translate to sound, touch, taste, and smell. If something like that pops up, write it down and go back to visual information. Visual information includes such things as size, shape, color, spatial information, and activity. Descriptions based on the visual aspects of the subject of inquiry form the main part of the description of each primary information point.

It is important to understand the difference between *describing* and *labeling* an aspect of primary information. A label is usually a noun that attempts to identify what the aspect you are studying is. It is also a guess. For example, a liquid could be labeled as "lake" or "ocean." An object could be labeled as "mountain" or "house." Use of labels and guesses should be avoided when doing scrying. Most often these labels are inaccurate. Attempting to guess or identify what the subject is will destroy the integrity of the scrying session and shut down the scrying process. It is not just inaccurate—guessing is destructive to the session.

Sketching identifiable objects of the primary information in such a way that you tend to put a label on them is just as bad for the accuracy of the session as using verbal labels is. This is why drawing the outline of the primary information should be done, rather than drawing a symbol representing a particular object. Draw shapes and activity; describe using words, colors, and other aspects that cannot be sketched.

Shapes should be drawn whenever possible. Because some of you will want to do traditional scrying, it is very important to sketch the information as often as you can, whenever you are able. Even if you cannot draw well, the act of sketching strengthens the deeper-mind connection. Outlining the overall shape of the primary information helps avoid labeling. If you perceive something long, brown, and tall, don't draw a tree; instead, draw a couple of parallel lines close together and describe the impression as "brown" and "green." If you feel like there is a hard, solid, gray object, do not draw a building; instead, draw an outline of the shape you are perceiving and write the words "gray," "hard," "opaque," etc.

Picking Up Primary Information Aspects as You Go

As you work, you may find that you pick up a point of primary information that is not in the original square you made at the beginning of the session. If this occurs, you should write down that you perceived an additional point of primary information at that place in the session. When you finish with the square of primary information points you are working on, you can go back and work on the one you picked up during the scrying part of the session.

I suggest finishing one primary information square before starting on a new one. It keeps the session more organized when you do that. It is easy to lose track of where you are when you chase the additional primary information points before finishing the one you are on. As you gain experience with this system, you will gain more flexibility and be able to explore at will without getting lost. I recommend this only for the sake of organization. If you stay organized, your information will be easier to interpret.

Activity should be described, including actions, purpose, and focus of the activities you perceive. Spatial information should be sketched on a map. Spatial information is the relationship of one point of primary information in time and space to another point containing information. The opening of the session, where a square is drawn with the three points and the primary information is identified at those points, is the beginning of mapping the subject of inquiry. You can, if you wish, use a larger square and make a more detailed map with sketches, and descriptions next to the sketches.

Branching Your Session

We have gone over basic scrying with one box containing three aspects of primary information. If you want to work on having a more detailed session, then you simply add boxes as you progress through the session.

The second way of branching your information is to move to a different perspective. This is how it works. When you do your first box of primary information, the box represents a snapshot photo of the target location. You are studying aspects of that location by scrying. If you move to a different location, you will perceive additional aspects of that location. To do this, make a map of the target site. This is a separate sheet from the paper containing your session data so far (that is, the paper with your points of primary information and scrying data). The map with the points of primary information and their location in the square are kept separate from the rest of the scrying session data so that you can easily refer back to the map and the points of primary information.

This separate piece of paper is a map of where you are looking and does not have any points of primary information or scrying data on it. It is mostly an imaginary map. Write a small X at the center, which represents your first perspective and your first primary information box. Systematically move around by making an X to represent the new vantage points from where you want to look.

If you want to move to the right, then make an X at the place where you would stand if you were looking at the target. It's just like a road map—you make an X, move, and make another X. When you make a second X to the right, after you have moved, then label that X with a 2 so you know that it is the second perspective. Once you have done that, get out another sheet of paper and work as if you were starting a new session. You are not starting a new session, but every time you move your perspective, you begin with the three points of primary information in a new box, just like you did when you first started that session. After you have the three aspects, scry each aspect the way you do at the beginning of a session. When you finish scrying, you can move to another perspective and label it with an X, with a 3 by the X since this is now your third perspective. Repeat the box with the three points of primary information and scry those points.

You can continue this as much as you want. I have had sessions go up to forty pages. Also, you can go overhead in the air above the target or down under the target looking up. I usually scry from four or five perspectives. I start with the center, then move right, back to center, move left, back to center, go overhead, back to center, then underneath, and back to center. I return to center after each move so I do not get lost. It is really easy to lose your place doing this. Keep it organized when you work.

When Someone Asks You to Scry a Target and Gives You Too Much Information

If you have been practicing as instructed, it will irritate you to have someone give you a bunch of information about a target they want you to scry. Do not get mad at them. There is a way to work so you can get at least a little bit of good data in situations like this.

First, go for the points of primary information, stick with the session structure, and go for details that were not told to you. Dividing the task into unique questions can help you hide a target when too much information has been given to you. When you divide up the task, try to make at least four unique questions. Create the tasking statements and put them in a grab bag. Pull a statement and follow the structure outlined in this book. Doing this will help you derail the analytical process of your mind and get some good deeper-mind information. Continue to focus on sketches over verbal data whenever possible. Focus on the outline of the targeted area rather than drawing a recognizable object.

Handling Labels

If a label pops into your mind during this part of the session, write it down and save it. After you perceive a label, it is a good idea to intentionally break away from it. I use the following statement when I mentally break from a label: "This is not X (label). It could be anything. Return to X aspect of primary information and scry." Even if you sometimes guess labels correctly, they should still be broken down into descriptive terms or sketches in session. Using them and allowing them in the session as labels or guesses will eventually hijack your scrying and decrease the accuracy and quality of your work. The goal of the session is not to guess what the subject of inquiry is or what it contains, but to describe each primary information point using sketches and descriptive terms—mostly adjectives, verbs, and adverbs.

Once you have finished with the point of primary information where the label occurred, you can break down the label into descriptive terms. Do not do this until you have finished scrying that particular aspect of primary information. Write the label down and ask yourself, "How does this (label) resemble the target?" Then write down the descriptions of that label as they come to you. Usually you will find that the label itself is not accurate, but aspects of the description of the label are. This is called internal symbolism. The label is the analytical mind symbolizing the perceptions rising from the deeper mind.

In advanced scrying, rather than casting labels aside, you can break them down into descriptive terms; but for the beginner, it is more important to train the connection between the deeper mind and the superficial mind. Discarding the labels is preferable to teach the superficial mind to stay out of the way of the connection with the deeper mind. The natural tendency is to try to control, guess, and interpret the perceptions coming from the deeper areas of Spirit. This has to be avoided in order to do accurate scrying.

As you advance in skill, you break down the labels in terms of belief and descriptive terms. The belief is isolated from the session, and descriptive terms are added to the current description of the primary information point you are working on. For example, if you perceive what you believe to be a tree, the belief that it is a tree would be isolated and discarded from the session. The descriptive terms that would describe said tree ("brown," "gray," "black," "green," "hard on the bottom," "flapping on top," etc.) would be added to the description list of that particular primary information heading.

When these sorts of descriptions are examined during the feedback session, you will find that at least some of the descriptive terms used to describe the label are accurate, but they usually are not what the label is. For example, a "tree" label might turn out to be a tower with a green flag on it when the feedback is examined.

Example of an Internal Scrying Session

As an example, I will use the session referred to at the beginning of this chapter, which has these four possible targets: Eiffel Tower, White House, Cathedral of Notre-Dame, and Windsor Castle. Earlier I found these three points of primary information: *object*, *liquid*, and *object*. I will put these targets back into the grab bag and draw again. I cannot use the primary points I found earlier because I did the feedback session and revealed the target. Once the target is revealed, it is no longer hidden. I can, however, put the target back in the grab bag. There is a chance I could draw that target out of the bag again, but I will not know it until the end of the session. Doing targets more than once is not a problem. The information, when you repeat a target, is often more detailed and different in perspective. Each session will yield new information.

It is important that you do not consciously know which statement of intent you are scrying. It must be hidden. This point has been made before, but it cannot be emphasized enough. For this example of an internal scrying session, I will be using the same tasking statements for the grab bag from page 41. It is possible that I might draw the White House target out of the grab bag again. I have not eliminated it from the target pool.

I take a slip of paper out of the grab bag, set it aside, and draw my square on the paper, placing within it three evenly spaced points in a roughly triangular pattern. I perceive the following primary information aspects:

1. Object
2. Object 2
3. Presence

I write down these three points, each on a separate page since the notebook I'm using has small sheets. I am now ready to scry. Instead of scrying the target, I will scry these points of primary information. These aspects will be the focus for scrying, one point at a time. You can do one of two things: each point can have a separate sheet of paper, or you can divide your paper into sections, with each point having its own section.

I scry the first point, which is *object*. This is internal scrying, so it is an interaction in my mind with my imagination. I study the first object within my mind. I perceive a couple of right angles and the colors gray and black. I find it wet-looking, which is toward the bottom—darker on the bottom, with an uneven border. It is hard and opaque.

I finish that point, then on my next sheet of paper I write "object 2." This helps me avoid confusion between the two objects. In my imagination I go to the second object and describe it. I perceive "black, lacy, hard, metallic-looking," and the purpose feels "decorative." I have a label of "wrought iron fence." After scrying the second point, I break down that label into the descriptives "sturdy, horizontally oriented, layers, hard, black." This finishes the second aspect.

I move on to the third point, which is *presence*. I perceive "activity, orderly, disorderly rambling, bipedal, multicolored." I have a label of "military," which I break down into "black, gold, uniform, stately."

I have now finished my three points of primary information. Remember, these are just in my imagination and mind. I am not seeing any visuals during this session. This is strictly an internal mental process.

It is time for the feedback session. I open the slip of paper. My target is statement of intent number three, which is Notre-Dame Cathedral in Paris. The tasking statement is "Go to Notre-Dame Cathedral in Paris, France, and scry the buildings and surroundings at 1600 hours on June 20, 2020."

Let's look at the various perceptions. The first object had the colors gray and black, right angles with wetness on the bottom, hard, and opaque. This is consistent with the exterior of the cathedral, so it would be a hit. The second perception had a label of "wrought iron fence." Here is a good example of where you can pick up a label that is actually at the location. There is a wrought iron fence right in front of Notre-Dame Cathedral. The description information that resulted when I broke down the "wrought iron fence" label still applies, and gives quite a bit of accurate information about that structure. Even though I do perceive labels accurately at times, I still break them down and assume that they are symbolic and inaccurate. I still maintain the session structure. Even so, I always do a happy dance inside when I do feedback and find that I perceived an accurate label during the scrying session.

The third point of primary information is *presence*, and I have a number of perceptions here. Some entities are organized and some are rambling—this is consistent with the typical activity and appearance of Notre-Dame Cathedral. The "military" label, however, is probably not present at the cathedral. Usually a label is not accurate but is a result of mental processing. There may be a procession there that could be perceived as military, or there may not be. There is no way to know this. I would count the military part of the perception as a miss. The colors may be there, and there may be people in procession, but it is not verifiable at this time. Having unverifiable information in your session is normal. All sessions will have verifiable information and unverifiable misses. It is important to learn to be okay with this. Overall, the session was very good. The wrought iron fence was a bonus and a happy-dance kind of hit.

The target date in the tasking statement for Notre-Dame Cathedral was June 20, 2020. I went back to follow up on the feedback during the editing of this book, as the date in question was a future date in relation to the scrying session that was done in December of 2019. There was a question regarding the accuracy of the perceptions related to the label of "military" and the associated data that needed to be clarified for the feedback to be complete.

On that date in Paris and throughout Europe, there were protests related to the murder of George Floyd by a police officer during an arrest in the US. The protests spread to Europe, and on June 20, 2020, one of the largest protests against police brutality and racism was staged in Paris, France. There was violence and a confrontation with the police during the protest. I am fairly certain that the perception of " military" was related to the protests going on that day and, in fact, was not a miss. Instead, it turned out to be an unexpectedly accurate prediction of a future event. This shows the importance of doing thorough feedback after the date has passed and all the information can be obtained regarding the target on that day.

The overall session time was only about ten minutes. It took a little longer because of the process of writing the information down in two places in my notebook, one for the session record and one for this book.

How the Perceptions of Internal Scrying Feel

I think it may be helpful to describe what the perceptions feel like as you are doing internal scrying. It is a difficult thing to set down in words since it is a subjective experience. Generally, anything that comes to you that is descriptive is coming from the deeper mind. Internal scrying focuses on visual aspects, so the appearance, activity, and spatial information are the most important things you are looking for. This is not only scrying in its own right, but also prepares you for visual scrying. It helps develop a line to that deeper part of yourself that is needed to induce accurate visual scrying and casting.

Internal scrying feels a little like a daydream and a little like ordinary thinking. It does not really feel like it is real. You may have a sense of just making it up. Ideally you should feel a fair bit of doubt. Uncertainty is your friend. When you are unsure, it means that your thinking and analytical process are being derailed, which allows subtle perceptions from the deeper mind to come through. It does not usually feel like you know what the target is. The perceptions come in bits and pieces. You may feel like disregarding them. It is normal to be a little bit stressed and worried about whether or not what comes to you is correct. It is important at this point to realize that some of the information is going to be accurate and some is going to be inaccurate. If you can accept that, then you will be able to relax a bit and enjoy the experience.

Deeper-mind perceptions are soft and easily overwhelmed. They feel tenuous, and you have a feeling that you should just ignore them. The images that come across are fragments, bits and pieces, that do not seem logical. You have a sense that you do not know what is going on. By contrast, belief and expectation biases feel more certain. You have a strong impression that this must be it. It feels like these perceptions makes sense. The sketch is something you recognize. You have a feeling of connecting the dots. Perceptions that are a result of belief and expectation biases come across vividly and powerfully. They will tend to follow a logical sequence, like the plot of a story. A picture may appear in your mind and imagination, or even in the scrying speculum.

After you have had some experience with feedback sessions, you will become much more suspicious of the story lines and strong images that come to mind, and learn to pay more attention to the softer perceptions that come from the deeper mind. It is important to write down as much as possible so you learn which is which. The deeper-mind perceptions do not come across in a way you generally would expect.

Use of Meditation

I will say a few words about meditation and other traditional exercises. You do not have to meditate to do scrying. Meditation does not make you a better scryer. What it does is help you learn about yourself. When you go into meditation and look at images and perceptions, they are just as mixed with bias and intellectual interference as they are when you sit at a table with a piece of paper. In my opinion, the only way to learn which perceptions come from the deeper mind is to hide the statement of intention and scry blind to it. I have done it both ways. To me there is no comparison between the two.

Meditation does teach you how to quickly quiet your mind and keep your body still for a period of time. This is valuable when you learn to scry traditionally. External scrying, or scrying with a speculum, depends in part on physical stillness and good observational skills. However, no amount of meditation will replace practice in scrying itself.

Practice Sessions

What you should do at this time is work through several targets of a nature similar to the targets I have examined in this chapter. The sessions I wrote up here were actual sessions, not just examples. For your first sessions, I suggest that you do at least four sessions consisting of drawing the square and triangle and determining the primary perceptions of the target. You can do as many as you want. Internal scrying develops accuracy quickly for the majority of people. If you find that your first few targets are accurate and then you have a few misses, do not worry about that. This can be frustrating, but it is a normal stage of development. Just keep practicing and make sure to do feedback thoroughly. After a bit of time, things will even out and you will have a mixed bag of hits and misses, with a few more hits than misses.

Interpretation of Session Data

Once you have done your feedback and you know what perceptions are present, you can then interpret what was going on. I can tell by my data, in comparing it to photos of Notre-Dame Cathedral, that I was scrying the front of the cathedral, and I was looking down toward the ground when I did so. When I looked at my perceptions and compared the ones that I knew were present at the target site with photos, I could tell that the part of the stonework I was seeing is the water-stained bottom layer, and the wrought iron fence is right in front of it. The line of people waiting to get inside is also in that area. It is a very crowded area. The crowds and activity are attractive to the deeper mind, and given a big target like this, it will tend to focus where the action is.

In this target I had a label of "military" at the site. As I write this, this target is in the future, and I do not know what will be going on at the cathedral on the date and time written on the tasking statement. I cannot really do a feedback session on this part of the target right now. This will happen with moderate frequency when you scry. Some of the misses may be future events. So it is not a bad idea to keep a record of the scrying saved somewhere, and to take another look at these perceptions after the date has passed to see if there is any indication that this sort of presence was at the cathedral on this day.

Almost all sessions will have some data that you just cannot verify one way or another. For the beginner, unknown data needs to be eliminated as much as possible so that you can learn how your perceptions work and how they come across to you. You do not learn as much from unverifiable perceptions. This is why you should save the partially tangible and esoteric targets for later, after you have gained a foothold on that slippery, tenuous path that leads to the deeper mind. Even if you are experienced as a Tarot reader or familiar with other divination systems, I would suggest doing a few really well-grounded sessions until you get a feel for it.

Note on Expectation Bias When Interpreting the Session

It is a good idea to remember that you will be imposing mental expectation bias on your interpretation. Practice with grounded targets will help you be more accurate and less biased in your interpretation. I suggest staying away from targets whose results carry emotional energy for you while you are learning this skill. Right now you are learning how to see deep visual information. Scrying is using your mind in a way that you are not used to. It will take a few rounds to sort out how to focus and how the session flows and works for you. I believe most people will be able to pick this up quickly. When you are trying to interpret information, it also helps to have the aid of another person who is neutral emotionally with regard to the subject of inquiry. Addressing and avoiding bias as much as possible will increase your credibility as a seer.

CHAPTER FOUR
TYPES OF DOWSING

Dowsing was the first psychic skill I learned. I had always been fascinated with it, and I wanted to learn how to do it. It took me nearly twenty years to learn how to dowse in a way that is both objective and accurate. Dowsing is a helpful skill when you are scrying. It can be used to eliminate and clarify aspects of primary information quickly. It can also be used in stand-alone sessions. It is an easy-to-use, lightweight method of divination that is very practical and can be worked up to a decent level of accuracy. In this chapter I will cover several different dowsing techniques. Practice these techniques and use the ones that work well for you. For those who have trouble using the traditional tools, I have alternative methods that will work for you.

As with scrying, I was involved with a dowsing group designed to predict the outcome of two-team ball games. Predictions were done weekly. This dowsing team was part of Applied Precognition, an organization that did predictions using various techniques and measured their accuracy with scientifically accepted and objective methods of measurement. While I was doing this work, I developed my personal toolbox of dowsing techniques and had the opportunity to test and verify them under very strict conditions of measurement and tracking.

Pendulum Dowsing

Pendulum dowsing is most frequently used for locating things on maps. Maps can be geographical or representative of other objects such as the human body. In chapter 5 I will go over pendulum dowsing using charts, maps, and other graphic tools. I have a unique approach to pendulum dowsing, so it is important that for the moment you disregard any information you may have learned previously regarding this type of dowsing.

Pendulum dowsing is suitable for scrying sessions. It will help you save time and effort, as it can provide quick answers to questions you have while you are working through a session. Pendulum dowsing is also better suited for maps than dot matrix or rod-type dowsing techniques are.

A pendulum can be made from just about anything that can be dangled at the end of a thread. Commonly used tools are miniature plumb bob–type devices, which are usually made of silver, brass, crystals, or wood. My personal preference, and the best for doing stealth work, is a sewing or darning needle and a length of fine sewing thread. The best thread to use does not tangle too easily but is fine enough that you cannot really feel it between your fingers while you are working. A pendulum for divination or map work should feel almost weightless. Ideally you should not detect the texture of the string or thread against your fingers when doing this kind of dowsing.

If you have naturally steady hands, then you will have more difficulty with pendulum dowsing. The solution is to use a lighter pendulum and a finer thread. Do not use a chain. I take the chains off the divination pendulums I buy the minute they come home. The pendulum itself should be lightweight and give a minimal sense of movement and weight at the end of the thread. A small lightweight pendulum is a better tool for working on small charts, graphics, and maps.

For discreet pendulum dowsing, I recommend a needle. If you carry a sewing kit, a needle and thread taken from it are perfectly adequate. You can also use a car key, a ring, or other small jewelry items. The thread holding the pendulum should be about four inches long—you do not want a long string when doing maps, charts, and graphs. If you are working outdoors, then the equipment has to be a little different. This setup is not suitable for outdoor work.

How to Use a Pendulum

When you are learning to use a pendulum, the first thing to do is to test and see if it will work for you. You determine whether you can use a particular pendulum by dangling it with the thread held between your thumb and index finger. You want about four inches of thread extending from your fingers to the pendulum, and a bit more to hold onto between your fingers. Try to hold the pendulum still and look to see if it moves or trembles. If it moves when you hold it, you can use it. If it stays steady when you hold it, then you need a lighter thread or a lighter pendulum.

The steadiness of your hands determines the best pendulum for you. I am a nurse, so I have worked with my hands my entire life and I have a very steady grip. I have to use a pendulum that I cannot feel at all when doing graphs. The thread has to be so fine that I cannot feel it in my hands, and the pendulum light enough that I cannot tell if I am holding it or not.

Pendulums work due to what is called the ideomotor effect. There is a natural tremor that develops when you try to hold your hand steady for a period of time. The muscles in your hands need to be tightened and slightly fatigued when you do this to activate the effect. The deeper mind can control the general direction and other aspects of the tremor. This happens without your conscious awareness. You cannot control this tremor consciously. You have to train your deeper mind to give a response, and use your body to move the pendulum to communicate that response. The "idea" part of *ideomotor* needs to come from the deeper mind. We will discuss how to eliminate the idea coming from the superficial mind. The "motor" part of *ideomotor* refers to the tremor. It is a subtle effect, and the movement coming from this can be very small. The pendulum does not swing wildly. Most of the time the movement is a vibration or small circles. When doing scrying or dowsing, always watch for subtle motion and subtle perceptions. These subtle impressions are usually more accurate and come from the deeper mind.

To train your mind and body to respond using the pendulum, you need to practice a little with it first. This requires fifteen minutes to half an hour. As you practice with the pendulum, you will learn to observe and understand how the response works. It is done more by observation than by intentionally moving the pendulum the way you think it should go.

When you first start to work with a pendulum, you have to make it move intentionally to start the dowsing process. It does not matter how you move the pendulum so long as the movement is regular. Some people move it in a circle, and others back and forth. The motion must be natural to you rather than a forced response. The observation of the movement is more important than trying to create a specific movement that may or may not be natural to you. This kind of training is one reason why people fail at using the pendulum. Oversimplified, specific forced-response training does not work for everyone. I teach observation rather than trying to elicit a specific and possibly unnatural response. My own pendulum technique started with a specific forced response, but then I realized that the accurate responses were different from the trained response. I started working with a more natural technique and found that the accuracy in my team-predictive work improved.

This is the natural response technique. You hold the thread and bring the moving pendulum over the target. On the correct response to your inquiry, you will observe a change in the action of the pendulum. Note how it changes. Do this intentionally for learning purposes by setting up something like a couple of playing cards or Tarot cards, and name one of the cards as a target. For this observation and only for this observation, you will know which card is your target, and you will be looking at the two cards in front of you faceup.

Swing the pendulum slightly so that it moves rhythmically. Take it over the non-target card and watch it. Then go over the target card and observe the change in its motion. Do this a couple of times and you will know how your pendulum is going to respond when it is over the target. Now you can work with hidden targets.

Pendulum dowsing is more a matter of learning what kind of response you are going to have rather than forcing a response. By a forced response, I mean a specific, predetermined movement of the pendulum from side to side, or back and forth, or circling either clockwise or counterclockwise. You can train a forced response, but it takes a longer time and sometimes is not as reliable as observing your own natural pendulum dowsing response. It is the fine hand movements that cause the pendulum to move, and it is through these that the dowser receives information. The sensation you feel is that you are holding the thread tightly and trying to stay steady, but the pendulum is still moving. It feels like something else is moving the pendulum because you are trying to hold it still. Some people even brace their wrist when dowsing to try to keep still. I do this only when I'm working over a small area so that I keep the dowsing precise.

Some dowsers will tell you that you need to ask permission to dowse. I do not do this. Your deeper mind is a part of you, and you do not need permission to access the information there, nor do you need protection from it since it is a natural part of your own being. No one but you is in control of that access. There are no psychic police patrolling and preventing anyone from accessing whatever information they want to access. You are in charge of your deeper mind and your personal energy. There are no limits to knowledge other than what you make up in your mind. It is better to work with this understanding of the truth than to pretend there are arbitrary knowledge limits that only gods and angels know.

Dot Matrix Dowsing

Dot matrix dowsing is easier to learn than pendulum dowsing in most cases. You need only a pen and paper. The question you dowse must have two possible outcomes. It can be a yes-no question, or it can be something like increase-decrease, above-below, left-right, past-future, or greater than-less than. When doing dot matrix dowsing, it is can be helpful to have several questions prepared for the session. It is preferable to use the grab bag system for dowsing questions as well as scrying. Randomly selecting the hidden questions using the grab bag method helps to decrease the possibility of error due to belief bias.

If there is only one question to be asked, then as long as the dot matrix dowsing is done properly, the issue with belief bias should be minimized. This is one of the reasons I prefer dot matrix to pendulum dowsing when the tasking cannot be hidden. It is much harder to skew the answer with dot matrix dowsing. There is a reduced danger of intellectual bias with this method. If you cannot hide the target, then you should use the dot matrix dowsing technique.

Dot Matrix Dowsing Technique

This dot matrix dowsing technique was inspired by a Hoodoo divination technique involving dice. Originally it was a form of numerology divination using gaming dice. I modified the technique and developed it into a dowsing method. It is a combination of the evolution of this method and a dowsing technique based on tapping or drumming. Dot matrix dowsing is very easy and can be done in a couple of minutes, either during a scrying session or as a separate session.

Focus on your primary information point from the session, or on the paper you drew out of the grab bag. Draw a square on a small sheet of paper and divide it into four smaller squares by making an equilateral cross through its center. Quickly, without thinking about it, tap the area around the cross with your pencil so that you create a random cluster of dots in each square. Do not count the dots as you are working, and focus your eyes somewhere other than on the paper. You are basically using the pencil as a drum on the paper. All the squares need to have marks in them. The tapping should be rhythmic and briskly done. You should work in this way for less than ten seconds.

When you finish, count the number of dots in the four parts of the square. If the total number of dots in a square is even, then the answer is yes. The square is a "yes" square. If the total number of dots in a square is odd, then the answer is no. The square is a "no" square. The purpose of drawing the cross is to provide for uncertainty in the answer. If two sub-squares give a "yes" response and two sub-squares give a "no" response, then the answer is uncertain or "maybe." When asking a simple question that can be answered only by a "yes" or a "no," without the possibility of a gray area or "maybe" response, it is the total number of dots in the whole square that should be noted.

The assignment of values can be something other than yes-no. Dowsing can indicate things like increase-decrease, above-below, left-right, or past-future. These can be assigned according to the needs of the subject of inquiry. Generally speaking, an even number of dots is positive and an odd number is negative. When you start with an assignment of the even or odd numbers to a certain value, that assignment should not be changed. Keep its association with even or odd. The more you work with this, the stronger the associations become and the more accurate the dowsing. For example, if you use "left" as an odd number of dots and "right" as an even number, then keep those associations the same when you work your sessions. Do not change them from session to session.

Both scrying and dowsing session setups have a cumulative effect. Session mistakes and successes affect future sessions. Even if the future sessions are done with good technique, errors in the past can still hijack present and future work. I cannot explain why this is the case, but it is an observation I have made over the years. The cumulative effect of poor technique lasts for about three months after corrections are made.

I prefer dowsing methods where your subconscious has control over the process. Accuracy in dowsing depends more on connecting with your deeper mind than on synchronicity. A deliberate method such as dot matrix dowsing is more accurate than random throws of the dice or drawing a few cards from a pack, because the deeper mind controls the production of dots on the paper through your body. A method like the dice throw is dependent on synchronicity, or the forces of the universe, to provide the answer to the query. This kind of work does sometimes provide accurate answers, but the locus of control is external. You are saying in essence when you roll the dice that "God, gods, angels, or saints are providing me with the answer." I prefer an internal locus of control that believes that "I am responsible for my deeper mind, and I can access any and all information through it." It does not mean that I do not believe in divinity or divine beings. It means that I believe that the universe functions in such a way that everything anyone will ever need can be found in the deeper mind. That access is unlimited and it is free. It cannot be restricted. Access to it is the heritage of humanity and other intelligences given freely without cost.

Other creatures are also able to access the deeper mind according to their ability. The reaction of a dog or cat to the paranormal is one example, and their mysterious behavior of waiting for a family member at the door when that person starts for home out of the creature's sight, smell, and hearing is another. We see the result of their perceptions but often do not realize that they are accessing the same thing we do when we go to the deeper mind for information and wisdom.

When experimenting with dowsing, I have found that the most accurate methods rely on obscuring the inquiry or the answer in some way and creating a deliberate connection with the deeper mind. An advantage of the dot matrix technique is that it does not depend as much on the ideomotor effect, so those who struggle with a pendulum can easily use this method, as well as tapping.

Dot matrix dowsing obscures the answer from the superficial mind since you work faster than you can count. The subconscious, or deeper mind, can count regardless of the speed, putting it in control. It is the superficial mind that interferes with the information coming from the deeper mind. Synchronicity methods have inconsistent accuracy when put to a test with strict accuracy measurements and tracking.

Tapping

Tapping is used mostly with linear graphs (X graphs) and XY graphs, charts, and maps where multiple dowsing hits may be needed to give a prediction over time or to find multiple artifacts on a map.

This technique is very vulnerable to belief and expectation biases. The target has to be hidden in some way when you are doing this technique. This works best when you use tapping in a scrying session where your subject of inquiry is hidden and you are working on clarifying primary points or studying the target over a span of time. I will go over this in more detail in chapter 5.

Tapping is a good technique to work into your session in order to find timelines, bigger or smaller, and other parameters that can be graphed on a linear graph or XY graph. The blank graph is drawn on a sheet of paper, and you tap a pencil around it. A line is drawn through the thickest concentrations of dots. Your mind needs to be slightly distracted while you do this. The method will be presented in the next chapter.

It is a sense of feeling things out with the pencil while you tap. Tapping is done in a rhythmic drumming manner, and since clusters of dots are used instead of specific numbers of dots, it can be done for longer than ten seconds. I usually end up tapping for about thirty seconds when I do an XY graph or map.

This method took its inspiration from Sámi rune drumming. This is a traditional shamanic divination using a specially marked drum. An indicator, which is a bone or stone, moves across the surface with the beating of the drum until it reaches a certain area of the drum that gives the divination answer. I modified this ancient aboriginal technique to use for dowsing.

Field Dowsing

Field dowsing is using dowsing techniques to find water, artifacts, minerals, and ores. It is also used for finding good gardening sites, burial locations, ley lines, and occult energy power points. Field dowsing is usually done outdoors. A form of dowsing rod or a pendulum is usually employed in field dowsing, although there is a type of outdoor dowsing called environmental scrying that uses no tools but relies on observing subtle changes in the air.

In outdoor dowsing and environmental scrying, the target may not always be hidden. If you are looking for something buried in the ground, then you have some hiding, which helps prevent guessing and bias. Learning how to dowse with rods takes practice, with the material you are looking for placed on the ground where you can see it. A wheel-spoke pattern is the usual search pattern. You take a section of ground and walk across it with the rod or other dowsing tool, then crisscross your path until you have created a pattern that is like the spokes of a wagon wheel, before moving on to the next section of ground.

Environmental scrying can be incorporated into field dowsing. Basically you look for a kind of heat wave that indicates where the target is. It is a subtle change of visual perception. It reminds me of looking for auras. It's best to work with the sun at a low angle when you do this, as direct sunlight will make the effect more generalized or related to heat rising from a dark surface. Environmental scrying is described in greater detail in chapter 7. It can be done separately or with dowsing.

Next I will discuss the traditional dowsing tools for field work. Even though your sessions may be indoors, there are times when you may want to go outside to do some work. Field dowsing works in tandem with environmental scrying, and the two skills should be studied and used together. Have fun with the outdoor projects. You will find them refreshing and enjoyable if you relax and do not worry too much about the results. They are good excuses to go outdoors and play around with a project.

L-Rod

The L-rod is a tool used for outdoor work once the mapping phase has been done. It is called an L-rod because it is shaped like the capital letter *L* tipped on its side. L-rods are usually made of metal. Coat hanger wire is the most frequently used material. Two rods are employed, one for each hand. You hold them in your hands by the short part of the L. The long portion of the rod should be about twelve inches long, or three times the width of your hand. If you have larger hands, then you need to make a longer rod. The length of the short section is less important, but its end should project below your hand about an inch. These rods can be purchased, but you need to maintain the ratio of the width of your hand to the length of the long section of the rod for the rod to work properly. I found this out through experimentation. It seems to be the best proportion to work with.

The rods function on the same principle as the pendulum. The rods are held loosely in the hands by their short segments, with the long segments pointing forward over the tops of your curled index fingers. The tips of the rods will either separate or cross when you step over the target. They can also both point simultaneously in the direction you need to go to move toward the target. The natural ideomotor effect has to be trained when working with the L-rod. The skill requires observation, knowledge of how the rods react over a target, and a forced response training to instruct the deeper mind how the information is to be conveyed. When you train the response, you reduce accuracy. It is not as reliable a method as observation alone, but you need to do some of this forced movement training for the rods to work outside, in the field. The movement of walking and bouncing around, especially on rough ground, obscures the more subtle movement of the rods.

Intentionally training the response to work a certain way results in a stronger action of the rods. Accuracy will improve with practice. Some people can go out and do it right away, and with others it takes practice, but everyone can learn the skill. The idea is to try to keep your hands steady while walking, and follow where the rods point. The rods need to be held loosely. Some rods have tubular handles that allow the rod to turn freely, but I find that I need to have direct contact. My L-rods are just old wire coat hangers cut into an L shape.

In order to train the ideomotor effect to show you what you want to find in the field, you need to practice by intentionally moving the rods in the way you want them to go. I practiced with a coin in the living room and the driveway. I made the rods point toward the item as I approached it and then cross when I stepped over it. Eventually it began to happen without me consciously controlling it. When you do this form of dowsing, you keep your elbows tight against your body to create a bit of fatigue in your arms. You do not squeeze the rods, but you do hold your hands and arms tense without maintaining a tight grip on the handles of the rods. The rods should be able to rotate freely in your hands.

This starts out as a forced response technique, and it takes some practice before you see a response that is disconnected from conscious effort. It is not ideal for doing chart and graph sessions since it requires you to move around and use a fairly large and conspicuous tool. The L-rods are good for outdoor work. The pendulum is too sensitive in the wind, and the paper-and-pencil methods are not practical while walking outside.

Y-Rod

The Y-rod is a very old, traditional tool that is most often used for finding underground water. As the name implies, it is a piece of wood that has the shape of the capital letter *Y*. The two ends of the Y are held in the hands, and the single leg points forward. The wood should be thick and stiff enough to offer resistance when the two ends are pressed toward each other, but springy and alive.

The rod is cut from a living branch and is usually cut by the dowser. The preferred woods are willow and alder, two types that grow in or near water. Fruit tree branches such as apple or cherry will also serve. The branch needs to be green when it is used—that is to say, it needs to have sap flowing through it. The branches of the Y-juncture need to be flexible. The bark is left on to keep it green as long as possible. I prefer willow for this, as it does not stain your hands. Alder has an unpleasant stain that is hard to remove. Apple and sugar maple also work for me. The Y-rod can be used for things other than finding water, but the size of the tool makes it impractical for using indoors with a map. I prefer the L-rods to the Y-rod for outdoor work.

As you approach the target, the extended end of the Y-rod will begin to vibrate, twitch, or move either upward or downward. The significance of the direction of movement is subjective and depends on the dowser, but it is more often down than up. When you reach the target, there will be a strong vibration of the rod. If you back away from the target, which is usually not visible, the end will begin to relax and level out. Accuracy depends on practice and observation. Dowsers who have extreme movements look good on YouTube but are not any more accurate than someone who has a more subtle response.

A Y-rod also creates a pulling sensation in the direction of the target, and may feel like it is changing position in your hands when you are over the target. For most people, this is a subjective sensation, and it may or may not be visible to an observer.

Learning the Y-rod and L-rods requires practice. For purposes of practice, the object you want to dowse should be intentionally placed in plain sight on the ground. The tool is then manipulated in a deliberate way to find the object. This is a different process than with the hidden target that we usually use. It is only for training purposes, in order to learn to manipulate the rods. Once the movement of the rod feels automatic, then you will use the hidden target system. Most outdoor targets are buried in the ground and are pretty much hidden anyway. You do not know if the target is where you are searching. This usually creates an adequate level of uncertainty to derail the analytical mind and expectation bias, especially if you miss a few times.

Bobber

A bobber is a long, thin branch that can be slightly weighted at the end with a fishing weight. If it is not weighted, then the thin part of the branch is held so that the thick end will provide a little bit of weight. The branch must be green, thin, and flexible. Once it dries out, it loses much of its spring and cannot be used anymore.

The rod dances up and down, here and there, as you walk with it. The bobber works by a pulling feeling toward the target. It is in constant motion, which makes it easier for some people to use than the Y-rod or L-rods. The motion is caused by walking. The bobbers I have seen are made from green first- or second-year pussy willow branches. The branch has to be long and very thin. Birch will work if you find a young tree with thin branches, as will a young maple. I have seen a mechanical contraption that looks like a fishing rod with a spring in it. I do not use such odd things for dowsing. There is plenty of willow growing around where I live. It's free and it works just fine.

The bobber is held in one hand and the end is allowed to bounce around. It will have a pulling feeling, which is usually subjective and not observable by others who might be watching. For most people it will be a subtle feeling. The feeling of the pull will change when you are over the target. You should practice getting the feel of the bobber by using a target placed in plain sight on the ground. Walk toward and away from the target, and try to feel slight differences in the pull of the branch. As with scrying, when you do actual dowsing work, it is important to hide your intended target whenever possible.

I encourage you to experiment with these dowsing methods and find one or more that work for you. Experiment with various materials as well. Dowsing, like scrying, is an art. There is quite a bit of variation between people with regard to the technique or tool that works best.

Coping with the Burden of Pre-session Knowledge

At some point in your practice, there will arise a situation where you cannot hide the target and you need to try to scry or dowse it. I want to discuss a couple of strategies for coping with this when it arises.

The first strategy is to refuse to do the inquiry. I worked with remote viewing circles for a couple of years while I was developing more effective scrying techniques. Most people in those circles will refuse to consider doing a target that is front-loaded. *Front-loading* means that you know what you are trying to remote-view. A small number of groups or clubs will train for very limited front-loading at the advanced level.

A second strategy is to train for a knowledge burden. Working with an increased information load is something you can train for. Initially you can start with just one aspect of general information, such as knowing that the target contains a living entity, the target is an angel, or the target is a flying object.

When you have the information, the first thing that tends to happen is that you try to guess what the target is. To counter this, it is a good idea to increase the number of possibilities in your grab bag. I would go to at least ten targets of interest in the bag. For me, this will effectively derail guessing enough for me to focus on the primary aspects. You then work the session in the same way you usually do with the points of primary information. The idea is to take your focus off the pre-session information and focus on the aspects of primary information. When you train for this, use grounded targets so you can do effective feedback.

If you are doing occult scrying, you have to train for pre-session information burdens. This is especially true if you are working with systems that require sigils or correspondences with astrological, elemental, or other parameters. The training for occult scrying has to be done with physical targets that are well grounded, having mostly known information. Your accuracy level has to be established before experimenting with a knowledge burden. It is also essential to know your strengths and weaknesses prior to the session. For example, you may have great accuracy with colors but be weak in determining timelines.

As you work with this, note how much pre-session information you can have before you start going on a trip to fantasyland. It is important to keep detailed records and to feedback the sessions very carefully so that you become aware of your personal tendencies when carrying a knowledge burden. Be aware that the knowledge burden will make your session more difficult. You cannot be emotionally tied to the results of your feedback when you work with pre-session information. You need to go back to working hidden targets when you start getting annoyed or frustrated.

Scrying a Known Target

Scrying a known target is one of the most challenging things in scrying that you can attempt. You will constantly be trying to push away from your biases. It takes strong focus and the ability to work very quickly to be effective at this kind of session. Speed is a major factor in working accurately with a contaminated session.

The strategy that seems to work best is to look for aspects of primary information that are unknown, and focus completely on these, with strong mental exclusion of anything else. If you maintain a passive mind, you will drift into belief bias. Once you fall into this trap, the session is done. Scrying a known target is like walking a tightrope, and you need to have excellent focus and be able to work very quickly to do it at all.

If you get anything correct in this kind of session, then you are doing well. Usually you will have a good perception or two, then experience rapid deterioration, which will also adversely affect your work with hidden targets. If you experience deterioration, you will need to work a recovery routine to get back up to par. The recovery involves resting for a month or so, then restarting with hidden targets until you are back to your baseline accuracy level. Targets must be grounded for recoveries. Feedback accuracy and attention to detail are critical.

Dowsing with a Known Target

Dowsing is a little easier to do with a known target because the situation almost always has aspects that are hidden from the dowser. This is especially true of field dowsing. The target may or may not be in the area you are searching. With field dowsing there is usually good and immediate feedback, which helps prevent deterioration of the dowsing ability.

The lack of immediate knowledge about the dowsing target adds a bit of doubt, and this doubt is the dowser's mental shelter from the aggressive belief biases and fantasies that attack you when you are aware of what you are looking for. Take shelter mentally in your doubt and uncertainty. Whenever you are dowsing or scrying, doubt and uncertainty are your best friends and your protection against the ravages of fantasy and bias. They are your guardian angels and the bridge to the vast knowledge and wisdom of the deeper mind. They are your lovers, your sword and shield. Always look for them, and to them, if you carry a pre-session burden of knowledge.

CHAPTER FIVE

USES OF DOWSING

Dowsing is a very useful tool when you are scrying. It will save you time and effort and help you focus on things that are important. Dowsing can quickly and objectively answer certain types of questions. It can be used to locate things on maps, charts, and graphs or in physical locations. Almost every scrying session I do involves dowsing at some point. Dowsing can also be used on its own and is great for a quick session. It gives good information in a very short period of time.

The techniques I teach are ones that anyone can use. I hope the information here will be helpful to those who have undeveloped abilities. Everyone can dowse, and like scrying, it is just a matter of finding the technique that works best for you.

Ways Dowsing Can Be Helpful

Dowsing allows you to focus on those aspects of the subject of inquiry where a later scrying will be most productive. It helps you avoid chasing dead-end targets. Dowsing can also be used to double-check perceptions while you are still in session. You can inquire about the accuracy of any perception during your session before the target is revealed. I will sometimes use dowsing to screen targets to be sure they contain enough information and are not based on fantasy or a hoax. If I need to know a location on a map, I use dowsing for this. If I need to make a graph or work with numbers, I incorporate dowsing into those sessions. Dowsing can also be used as a stand-alone session.

Dowsing is a good way to verify that you are scrying what you need to scry. During the session you can ask, "Have I covered the most important and requested information on this point?" This helps alert you if your scrying went off target. At the end of the session I usually dowse the entire session itself by asking, "Did this session cover the most important aspects of the statement of inquiry?"

These are just a few examples of how to apply dowsing in a scrying session. Dowsing is done with a hidden target whenever possible. However, there are some types of dowsing that cannot be done as a completely hidden target. The issue with expectation and belief biases still holds true, and the risk increases with conscious knowledge of the target regardless of the divination method used. It is a good idea to have multiple targets prepared for the dowsing session and to use the grab bag technique whenever it is practical. Dot matrix dowsing, a technique that was covered in chapter 4, is the least vulnerable to bias and should be used when the target cannot be hidden.

Yes or No

Most of the questions answered by dowsing are binary questions. These are questions with only two possible responses. Examples of binary response sets are such things as correct-incorrect, yes-no, higher-lower, right-left, more-less, and longer-shorter. Handling simple binary questions by dowsing the answer during a scrying inquiry can help the scryer save time and effort.

The most common type of binary inquiries are yes-no questions. These are usually screening questions for the subject of inquiry that is to be scryed. For example, when scrying the prophecies of Nostradamus, I would screen the prophecies I wanted to investigate by asking if the prophecy was at least 50 percent accurate. If the answer dowsed was yes, then I would follow up by asking if the prophecy had been fulfilled.

Another example of a yes-no dowsing question is to ask if an object or photograph is a hoax, or you could put the question another way and ask if it represents a real event, object, or activity. A photograph or drawing of a cryptid, an animal that is alleged to exist but is not officially recognized, is an example of a good target for a dowsing inquiry. You could ask if this animal exists in the physical world.

Higher or Lower

Higher or lower is another common binary inquiry. In a higher-lower inquiry, a fixed starting point is set. If you are doing stock market predictions, for example, you would average out the previous year's values on the stock or index and use that for your starting set point. The set point for a higher-lower response should be the approximate average of whatever value you are investigating. Higher or lower responses usually involve numbers. They can also involve physical measurements such as depth, weight, height, the number of objects, and so on. The set point has to be arbitrary at times. This happens when the averages are not known or not relevant to the question being asked. The higher-lower dowsing inquiry can be variable. In that case, you should set up the inquiry on a number line (which will be described shortly), or multiple elimination inquiries can be made.

Example of Higher or Lower Dowsing

Let's say I am asked to dowse and compare the height of two mountains, Mount Everest and K2, to determine which one has the greatest elevation above sea level. There is some controversy over the altitude measurements of these two mountains. Because the target is specific, I cannot obscure the general inquiry. To obscure the targets, the names of the two mountains are written on identical cards, placed facedown, and mixed up so I cannot see which mountain is written on which card. This is another obscuring technique, and it is a very fast and simple way to hide the objective. In this case, two index cards are used.

I then write my tasking statement: "Go to K2 and Mount Everest and determine which mountain is higher and which is lower than sea level. Indicate the answer by the pendulum."

The pendulum responds strongly over one of the cards. I turn over the cards and find that the pendulum indicates that the higher mountain is Mount Everest. Feedback suggests there is a good possibility that this is an accurate dowsing session. Tradition and most measurements indicate that Mount Everest is higher than K2.

More or Fewer

More or fewer is usually used in the same way as higher or lower inquiries. Counting objects in a scrying session is a common use for this parameter. Let's say you have multiple large square objects that you perceived in a scrying session, but you aren't sure of their number. You can count the objects using dowsing. You need to make your set point, or starting point, the number of objects you sketched on the paper during the scrying session.

Gray Area Dowsing: The Number Line

Binary dowsing, where there are only two possible choices, yields a black-and-white response. Sometimes you need to dowse a question where there is a possibility of a "maybe" response, a gray area where neither "yes" nor "no" could be completely correct. Number lines are a method for dealing with gray area questions, whose responses do not fall strictly into a yes-no division. A number line is just a line drawn on paper to represent a range of numbers. One end of the line indicates the low end of the range, and the other end indicates the high end.

I usually use percentage as my parameter with this type of inquiry. For example, if a prophecy has some aspects that are accurate and some that are not, you can ask for the percentage of accurate information in the prophecy. You would draw the number line and make 50 percent your center mark. One end of the line would indicate 0 percent, and the other end 100 percent. You would then dowse the approximate percentage of accuracy of that prophecy. This is a good way to check work that is obscure, like that of Nostradamus. If a quatrain falls below the 50 percent mark, it may not have enough accurate information to be worth scrying.

There are many gray area dowsing inquires that can be made. I will go over basic categories later in this chapter. Generally, gray area dowsing needs to be done with a pendulum or by tapping. As you will remember from the previous chapter, tapping is where you drum the paper with the tip of a soft pencil to make marks, and the area where there is the greatest cluster of marks indicates where the "yes" response is.

Hiding Number Lines and Graphs for Dowsing

Hiding dowsing targets is the best way to get accurate dowsing responses. Here is a technique that can be used to cover graph and number line types of target.

To hide your number line target, cut two separate pieces of paper into equal-size squares. One paper will have your number line, map, graph, or chart on it, and the other sheet will be a thick piece of completely opaque paper. Colored construction paper and artists' watercolor paper work well for this. When you draw the number line, graph, or map, do not draw it in the middle of the page or oriented the normal horizontal way you would write. Instead, draw it at an angle and off-center. This is to help you obscure the target somewhat. Once you draw your number line, graph, or map, you hide it by putting a thick sheet of paper of the same size and shape over it.

The two papers are then rotated against each other until you do not know which way is up or where the number line is located on the lower sheet. The top opaque sheet obscures the number line, forcing you to rely entirely on dowsing for information. You cannot guess—you must dowse for the data.

Once there is adequate uncertainty about where the number line, graph, or map is underneath the blank sheet that hides it, do your dowsing. Mark the place on the blank opaque sheet that comes up with a positive dowsing response using a pencil. Then, to mark the sheet of paper that has the number line (or graph or map), use a straight pin and pierce both sheets of paper where you made your mark on the blank top sheet. The mark will then be transferred accurately to the number line sheet below. It is important to puncture both sheets of paper. The puncture mark on the number line will almost never be directly on the line. I mark the area on the graph or map that is closest to the puncture mark. You will make several marks for the number line. There will be one that is close to the number line, and that is your answer.

When you do pendulum dowsing, dowse along a line diagonally from corner to corner of the blank upper sheet of paper, then dowse a line from corner to corner that begins on the opposite side of the paper so that the two lines cross in the middle and form an X (figure 5.1). Move the pendulum to the center of the paper and dowse an expanding spiral outward toward the outer edge. Work slowly and carefully. Mark on the paper any and all changes that you observe in the motion of the pendulum.

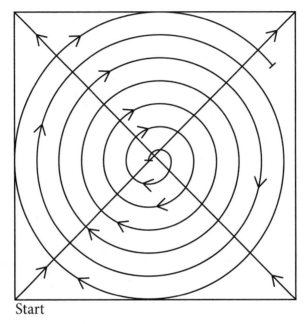

Start

Figure 5.1: Dowsing Search Pattern

If you are using tapping, then the areas with the greatest clusters of dots are the areas you need to mark and pierce with a pin to the paper that bears the number line. The pendulum responses need to be marked as you observe them, so you will be interrupting your pendulum dowsing to make a mark on the paper when the pendulum changes motion. The opposite is done if you are tapping. The clusters of dots from the tapping are marked and pinned after the entire search pattern is completed.

The pattern of the crossing X followed by the outward spiral starting from the center is a pattern commonly used in dowsing regardless of the method or the type of dowsing being done. There are other possible patterns. Generally, the dowsing search pattern needs to cover the entire blank sheet, and it needs to be systematic. Once you start working with a particular search pattern, it will help your accuracy to stick with it. I suggest that you try the X-and-spiral pattern. It is the one I usually use if I am pendulum dowsing, field dowsing, or chart dowsing.

You may end up with a couple of marks close to the number line or none at all. If the dowsing responses seem to avoid the number line as if it were repelling the pendulum, then the number line may not be dowsable as it is tasked at that time. Make changes to your tasking and try again after a short break. You can tell when you look at it whether the number line gives you the feeling that it is repelling the dowsing investigation. Most often there is a problem related to the tasking statement, or the number line contains fictitious information, and your deeper mind is trying to show you this through the dowsing perceptions. I have only had this happen a couple of times. Most of the time when I dowse, I have a couple of marks almost on the line, a few completely off the chart, and a few that are fairly close.

Using the cover sheet does not result in a perfectly hidden target, but it does reduce the vulnerability of the dowsing session to expectation and belief biases. The number line sheet is then added to my data for that session and is subject to feedback at the end of the scrying or when the time is completed for the prediction to have taken effect.

Maps

Scrying is very good for describing the area at a specific location. It does not, however, give you much to go on when trying to find that particular location. This is where dowsing with a map comes in very handy. A map usually contains a depiction of a specific geographical area. For map dowsing, you need to use a map that has substantial detail and exact scaling. A twenty-four-inch topographical trail map is usually what is used in professional remote viewing circles. You start out with a large map of the area in question. To do map dowsing, you need to use a pendulum and you need to hide the target. Pendulum dowsing is very vulnerable to belief and expectation biases.

The dowsing of the map is done after the scrying session is completed but before the feedback session starts. This is because it takes a bit of a different frame of mind to do map dowsing than to scry. Map dowsing is also done on longer projects that require more detail. In most cases it cannot be done in a fifteen-minute session. Map dowsing has to be meticulous in technique and is tedious. I prefer to save the tedious work until the end of the session. I usually need to rest a while after doing a map dowsing session.

To start a map dowsing session, take the portion of the topographical map you are working with and divide it into manageable square segments. These are drawn directly on the map with a pencil. The segments should be numbered. I usually start at the top left and work to the right, then after the top row of segments is numbered, I continue on the next lower row. These numbered segments have to be square, and if GPS is included on the map, each of your larger squares should contain an equal number of GPS coordinate squares.

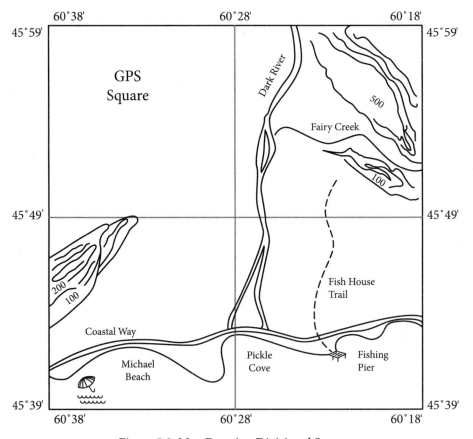

Figure 5.2: Map Dowsing Divisional Square

The GPS squares are defined by grid lines printed on the map that cross and divide the map into small squares (figure 5.2). You can tell if GPS coordinates are included on a map because these small squares will have numbers at the corners on large maps, or the numbers will be along the margins of smaller maps. These numbers refer to longitude and latitude.

I usually put sixteen GPS squares in one dowsing square if the original map is a large twenty-four-inch topographical trail map. The GPS squares in the dowsing divisional square are four across and four down, giving sixteen squares. If the map is in a book of maps that is about eight inches by eleven inches, then I put four GPS coordinate squares into each dowsing square. When I do personal work, it is usually with the smaller book of maps. The large twenty-four-inch topographical maps are becoming increasingly difficult to find.

Computer-based maps such as Google Earth are not acceptable to use in a serious or professional-level dowsing project. Accuracy with map scale ratio is important to accurate dowsing. I have found that the computer-based maps do not do an adequate job of maintaining scale, or at least that the translation between the map online and a printer changes the values and throws off the accuracy of the map. As computer printers and digital maps improve, it may be possible in time to produce a scale-accurate map using a digital online map and printer.

To dowse a map, a blank sheet of paper is placed over the square you have drawn in pencil on the map. On this paper you trace a square that is the same size as your dowsing divisional square. Remember, there are usually two kinds of squares on the map—the larger one is the dowsing square you have drawn in with pencil, and the smaller ones are GPS coordinate squares that are printed on the map. Do not confuse them. You must use very thin paper or tracing paper in order to see the square on the map clearly enough to trace it. It is critically important to accuracy that the map dowsing square and the square drawn on the blank sheet of paper be the same size.

In order to avoid expectation bias, you should work with at least four dowsing divisional squares for each project. The sheets of paper on which you traced the dowsing squares are labeled on the back in the same way as the dowsing divisional squares on the map. For example, if you label your dowsing squares on the map with "One," "Two," "Three," and "Four," then you would label the squares on the corresponding sheets of paper with a "One," a "Two," and so on. A minimum of four sheets should be used, but you may use more if you wish. Each label should be marked very lightly on the back of its sheet of paper so that when you are looking at the square you have drawn, you cannot see the label. You will be dowsing the blank square. It is important that you cannot tell at the time you are dowsing which map dowsing divisional square you are working on.

You can, if you wish, have margins around your blank squares on which to make reference lines or write notes. The blank squares, however, do need to be the same size as the squares drawn on the map. Instead of tracing the squares, you may find it easier to measure the size of the dowsing divisional squares on the map and then draw on separate sheets of paper squares of the same size. It is important to label both the map squares and the corresponding sheets of paper to avoid mixing them up.

To choose which blank square to dowse, place all the sheets of paper on the table with their labels turned downward and hidden, and mix the sheets up. Pick one at random so that you do not know which dowsing divisional square on the map you will be dowsing. Set the others aside, and when you finish dowsing the first square, continue with the remaining sheets until all of them have been dowsed. The labels should remain turned down and hidden until you have finished your dowsing project. If you have a large number of squares to dowse, you can divide the project into smaller, more manageable sessions. I recommend working for no more than thirty minutes at a time to avoid fatigue. On one of my projects I had to dowse fifty-four dowsing divisional squares, and I spread the work out over eight days.

Pendulums and tapping are the two methods of choice for map dowsing. The areas on the blank square you are dowsing that have a "yes" indication by pendulum or by tapping are marked by poking a hole through the paper with a straight pin. The pin mark or marks are transcribed onto the map after you have finished dowsing. This can be done by laying your blank square over the corresponding dowsing divisional square on the map and putting the pin through the hole in the blank square so that it touches the map. You then peel back the sheet of paper while holding the pin in place, and mark the location of the pin on the map with a small dot or X. To preserve the map, you do not pierce the map with the pin.

Map Dowsing by Elimination

Another method of handling map dowsing is by elimination. This helps narrow the search if you are uncertain about where to start. The goal of elimination is to start with a fairly large map and eliminate areas that are not related to the objective of your search. The technique of making a dowsing divisional square, copying the square onto a blank sheet, and labeling both the dowsing divisional square and the blank square on the paper with the same identifier should be used in elimination dowsing. As with map dowsing, a label should be on the back of each blank square, and the blank squares mixed up so that you do not know which dowsing divisional square on the original map you are dowsing.

The procedure for elimination is slightly different. In elimination dowsing, you do not know which area the target is in. You may have a large map, such as a map of a state or country. Start by dividing the large regional map into four sections. Draw the blank squares, then label and scramble the squares as in map dowsing. Dowse the four blank squares. Once you have dowsed the four squares, you can look at the labels and eliminate at least two dowsing divisional squares. You then take the remaining squares and divide each of these into four dowsing divisional squares. Continue using the same protocol until you have narrowed your search to an area of manageable size. It is normal to have more than one area come up with a positive response. If this happens, mark all positive areas and leave it at that.

When dowsing is done for mineral or archaeological purposes, a team of dowsers may be used, and there will be clusters of "yes" responses in areas of interest. Group dowsing rarely comes up with just one area of interest. The reasons as to why areas of interest turn up are usually revealed when the actual groundwork is done. If you have no positive response, and an area is strongly believed to be of interest, you can repeat the session after a space of time. Everyone gets odd responses and has runs of inaccurate dowsing. It is a normal part of the experience and is nothing to worry about. Feedback the session carefully. You will improve with practice and time. Map dowsing does require a bit of practice to get the hang of it.

XY Graphs

The use of an XY graph is almost always for advanced-level dowsing and predictive work. If it seems too difficult or complicated, you can skip over it for now and come back to it after you have acquired the basic skills of scrying and dowsing. However, you should read through the material in order to get a general sense of what is involved in graph dowsing.

An XY graph is a graph with two lines, one vertical line on the left side and one horizontal line across the bottom. The vertical line is labeled X and the horizontal line Y. This type of graph is most commonly used to track and forecast values and trends over time. When dowsing XY graphs, the horizontal Y line often indicates time and the vertical X line indicates the value that is to be predicted. A prediction of the change in the value of X over a period of time being examined, Y, is known as a trend. This method of chart dowsing can be used to predict things like temperature changes, weather trends, and health-related trends and changes.

The zero point, or starting point, of the graph is the lower-left corner where the X and Y lines intersect. Moving away from that intersection on these two lines usually indicates an increase of the value being measured for the X line and an increase or a progression in time for the Y line.

There are two basic techniques for dowsing this kind of graph that I will present here. I know four or five other techniques that are a bit more complex. The skills I am presenting here are the easiest ones and the most appropriate for the beginner. The two techniques involve the use of the pendulum and tapping. To set up an XY graph, you first sketch your graph, which can be done either before or during the dowsing session.

Session graphs require some explanation. If you are doing a scrying session and you perceive multiple presences and want to study how these presences change over time, you can use an XY graph to gain additional detail in that particular primary perception. For example, suppose that you detect three presences in an object. The object is moving and experiences destructive changes over a period of time. You sense that the presence density also changes during that period of time. You would then pick a time increment based on the perceptions of the overall time in which the destructive changes occurred (figure 5.3).

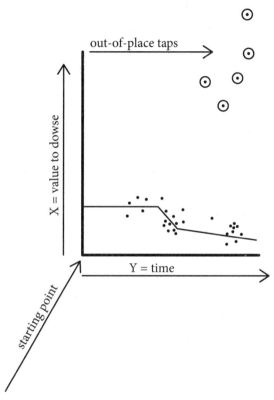

Figure 5.3: XY Graph

The division of time into increments of time on the horizontal Y line depends on what you perceive in the session. In this example, we will say it is a long period of time that is perceived, spanning several human lifetimes. You could divide your horizontal Y line into time increments of fifty years. If, on the other hand, you perceive in the session that the destructive changes occur over only a minute, then you could make the increments of time into seconds.

Use of the XY Graph with the Pendulum and Tapping

In the first method of dowsing an XY graph that I will describe, the XY graph is hidden behind a sheet of paper that is the same size and shape. The graph needs to be drawn fairly large for this kind of work. The graph and the covering paper are not rotated against each other. Proficiency with the technique needs to be mastered first before working with a disoriented graph. There will be some issues with expectation bias when you first start to do these kinds of graphs because of the lack of disorientation. Once you master the dowsing technique for this graph, then you can add the step of disorienting the graph by rotating it under the blank sheet of paper that covers it to help reduce the problem with expectation bias.

I usually make the graph five inches by five inches. The graph should pretty much fill the paper it is drawn on, with no more than a half-inch margin all around.

The dowsing pattern should be an X pattern with an outward-moving spiral that starts at the center. (See figure 5.1 for this search pattern.) This pattern is used for both pendulum dowsing and tapping. The X is made from corner to corner, going from the bottom of your blank sheet of paper to the opposite corner at the top. Any changes in the pendulum movement have to be noted with a pencil as you are working. If you are tapping, then tap the entire search pattern before marking where the clusters have fallen. This is the same procedure as for number line dowsing.

In XY graph dowsing, all the marks will fall within your graph, so you cannot get the obvious repelling effect that you do on a number line alerting you to the fact that your tasking statement is not applicable or is badly worded. For this reason, it is important that the tasking be something that is not fictitious, and it has to be worded properly.

Some of the marks will seem out of place. This is normal. Usually about 10 to 30 percent of the marks will not relate to the graph and will have to be discarded. This is true of both tapping and pendulum dowsing. There is no one method that is inherently better than the other. It is a matter of individual preference. I recommend working with both techniques until you achieve proficiency, as some situations will give better results with the pendulum and some with tapping.

The final step is to connect the dots. If a dot seems out of place, circle it but do not draw a line through it. Even though the dot is marked as out of place during the session, you do not know how accurate that judgment is until you do the feedback session.

The second method of XY graph dowsing is by tapping. For this technique you don't have to hide the graph—it is done directly on the XY graph. This works best in session when you have a hidden target. You need to tape the graph paper to the table so it will not move. Take a soft lead pencil and hold it lightly at the back end between your first finger and thumb. It does not matter so much how you hold it, but it is important to hold it lightly and loosely in your fingers. I hold the pencil like a drumstick. My motion when I tap is like playing a drum. Tap rhythmically over the graph area. Do not look at where you are tapping. You need the graph to be heavily covered in marks and you need to tap in a quick rhythm. Allow the dots to cluster. Work in this way for about a minute. The marks need to be well spaced in such a way that the entire time span is covered.

After you finish tapping, draw a line from the starting point of the graph that passes through the areas with the most dots and extends all the way to the end of the time span of the prediction. You draw the line from left to right through the areas where the dots are most densely clustered. The line is then your prediction. I like the tapping method more than pendulum dowsing for this kind of graph work.

Feedback is very important to do, and it has to be done over the time span that the graph covers. Predictive XY graph feedback will have to be done several times during the time period pertaining to the prediction. For example, let's say you have a stock that changes value monthly, and you predict that it will go up in value in one month, drop to half that value in two months, and go back to the original value in three months. At one month, two months, and three months, you have to do a feedback session on each of the predictions you made.

Alphanumerics

Alphanumeric values are letters or numbers. Dowsing is one of the best ways to perceive alphanumeric values. This can be done with graphs or with other techniques that I will cover in chapter 11. Dowsing is used in combination with scrying for best results. Alphanumerics are the most difficult objects to scry accurately. Employing dowsing with scrying will help increase your accuracy with this type of perception. Alphanumeric values must always be scryed or dowsed as a hidden or blind target.

Dowsing Charts

A dowsing chart is a graphic or pictorial arrangement of various related categories or values. It can be as simple as a circle divided into two halves by a vertical line, with one side marked with a "yes" and the other side with a "no," or it can be a complex pattern of many values.

I have seen quite a few dowsing charts. Mostly these involve health and other informational groupings. Health charts can have anatomical locations, acupuncture sites, or other information sets that are contained in a pie chart or semicircular chart, with a wedge-shaped section of the pie or semicircle marked to represent a specific piece of information. These charts work well in dowsing work, and you can easily make your own. However, they tend to be susceptible to belief and expectation biases. Pie charts are best used with a pendulum or with tapping.

Because of belief and expectation biases, the chart needs to be hidden from view while you are working. To do this, you need to trace or copy the chart onto a square sheet of paper. The chart must fill the entire sheet of tracing paper. Then use a heavy sheet of construction or watercolor paper that is cut the same exact size as the paper on which you traced the chart. This heavy paper covers and obscures the tracing paper that bears the chart.

Disorient yourself by rotating the papers against each other so that you do not have conscious awareness of the orientation of the graph under the obscuring sheet of paper. Then dowse and mark the "yes" responses with the straight pin as before. A square sheet of paper is used for this, because all sides are equal and you cannot tell which side is "up."

Statement of Intent for Dowsing

As with scrying, you need to write down a statement of intent that states exactly what you are dowsing for. The wording is very important for dowsing, as the accuracy of your session may depend largely on how well you word the tasking statement. Here are the requirements for a good statement of intent:

1. *Concrete:* The dowsing statement must be worded precisely and concretely. It needs to be very black-and-white. It has to be answerable (ideally) with one of two responses, such as yes-no, larger-smaller, heavier/lighter, or darker/lighter.

2. *Clarity:* Specific, clear wording is as important to dowsing as it is to scrying. Here is an example: "Go to and dowse _____. Is it higher or lower than the _____ set point?" There needs to be a command involving the words *go to* and *dowse*. When you are dowsing a chart, you need to command the deeper mind to open to the area that the chart represents, even if it is a symbolic or mathematical value, such as temperature or precipitation.

3. *Time, Place, and Goal Specifications:* It is important to specify time parameters, since your deeper mind can go to any point in time that ever existed or will ever exist. The location can be real or symbolic. When you dowse real places, the results will generally be more accurate. Goals have to be spelled out. For example, if you are looking to see if a prophecy has been fulfilled, make sure you specify which prophecy and the present time.

Example of Dowsing Statements of Intent

1. "Go to GPS coordinates 45N and 67W. Dowse and indicate any locations containing gold or silver ore in this area."
2. "Go to the Louisbourg Historic Area peninsula and dowse to indicate any hidden human remains dating from 1678 to 1778."
3. "Move through time to June 4, XXXX [put in the year that the game occurs], and dowse and predict the outcome of the baseball game taking place at Yankee Stadium. Home team is a positive response, and away team is a negative response."

Ideally the statements of intent should be hidden and drawn from a grab bag. It is not always as easy to hide the target for dowsing, since you have to work with a physical map of some kind most of the time. However, every effort should be made to at least scramble as much of the conscious information access as possible whenever working with perception. The more the target is hidden, the less of a fight you will have with your belief and expectation biases.

Feedback Session

Feedback for your dowsing session needs to be done as soon as you have the information. It takes a bit of time to build accuracy, and the only way that happens is by doing feedback. This is actually more important than good dowsing technique. To build accuracy, the targets need to be real time-space targets that can give accurate and detailed feedback. The typical trend in accuracy for dowsers is to have a really good start, then a run of inaccurate dowsing, followed by a gradual improvement. It is normal to have these runs of both highly accurate and very inaccurate work. Have patience with the inaccurate times, as things do eventually even out if you persist in doing concrete targets and good feedback sessions.

General Considerations

For the scryer, dowsing is a valuable skill to develop. You can do most dowsing using only a pencil and paper. I have included two pencil-and-paper dowsing techniques in the next chapter. Even if you are dowsing with tools, you do not need specialized or expensive equipment. With experience, you will find how to make your dowsing more efficient in the short time you have available. The basic skills of dowsing can be learned in less than an hour, but it does take a bit of practice to develop proficiency. Generally, the rule of thumb is that if something can be answered in one of two ways, it can be dowsed.

Gray area dowsing, with inquiries that can have more than two possible answers, adds information detail to your scrying sessions. I recommend that you put effort into reducing or confusing your conscious knowledge of the target as much as possible when you are trying to dowse. I have described a hiding technique in this chapter. For multiple dowsing inquiries of the same type, you can use the grab bag technique as well. For example, if you need to estimate dimensions, and you have three possible number lines of length, width, and height, then you can write your tasking statement for dowsing each parameter and toss all three into the grab bag.

In the scrying session, you do not need to reveal your target prior to doing the dowsing. You can dowse on the points of primary information as your focus, just like you do with scrying. The statement of intent is revealed after both the scrying and the dowsing are finished, then feedback is done on both sessions.

CHAPTER SIX

TWO CASE STUDIES

The following case studies are actual scrying inquiries I did in preparation for this book. They were done blind using the grab bag method. I did not know what the target was when I did the scrying or dowsing sessions. In these case studies I made notes about how I was feeling, problems with fatigue, and other factors that affected the scrying sessions. These notes should help practitioners gain a realistic understanding of how scrying works, what to expect, and how to handle problems that arise in session.

Scrying can be used to investigate visions of other seers as well as the lives of the seers themselves. The first case study presented here concerns one of the prophecies of Michel de Nostredame (1503–1566), better known as Nostradamus, a French seer who was a contemporary of the English Enochian magician Dr. John Dee. Nostradamus was a prolific writer who had many visions, which he recorded. He was both a scryer and an astrologer. My focus is on developing alternative techniques for studying his prophecies as well as those of other seers. The first case study here demonstrates the process I am using in this ongoing project. To fill the grab bag for this study, I selected prophecies of Nostradamus that are believed to still be unfulfilled.

As I have worked over the past few years through his various prophecies, as well as others by such seers as John of Patmos and Ezekiel, I have found that the prophecies tend to be focused on the home country of the seer and the time in which that seer lived. I have found occasional gems outside of these parameters. The prophecies give insight into the culture of the seer and the people at the time the vision took place. A scryer can investigate visions of other seers quite easily. It really is no different than working any other inquiry.

This type of target is one of my favorite kinds to do. It gives me not only information about the obscure prophecies I study but also insight into the life of the seer who made them. Time does not exist to the scryer. It does not matter that Nostradamus died hundreds of years ago. The quality of the results I achieve is very similar to what you see in group projects. The great thing about this kind of scrying is that anyone can do it. I am not special. This is just a skill I picked up along the way and am now passing on to you. I hope you have some fun with it because it can be very interesting.

Nostradamus's prophetic work is divided into groups called centuries. Each century has one hundred quatrains. A quatrain is a brief verse of four lines that Nostradamus wrote containing a cryptic description of the vision he saw. I rely mostly on the content of the quatrains plus my own investigations to determine whether or not the prophecies have been fulfilled. I have also studied modern authorities on Nostradamus. The modern writings have played a very small role in isolating quatrains that have not been fulfilled; however, I have been able to eliminate some of the ones that have already come to pass using a study of modern interpretations of Nostradamus's writings.

Nostradamus wrote in an older dialect of French. The English version of the quatrain scryed in this chapter is from *The True Prophecies or Prognostications of Michael Nostradamus*, translated by Theophilus de Garencières and published in London in 1672. The translation is meant only to give an idea of what the quatrain says and served as a reference for my scrying session. Remember, the focus of this work is the analysis done by scrying the vision of the scryer, not scholarly accuracy of the quatrain translation.

The quatrain that forms the basis for case study one is quatrain II.97.

Screening the Quatrains for Accuracy and Relevance

The first thing I did when I was looking for suitable quatrains by Nostradamus to use in the grab bag for this case study was to screen by dot matrix dowsing a number of quatrains to find several that were plausible prophecies and still relevant to our time. This screening was done by dowsing two questions on each quatrain. The quatrains that passed the screening were then assigned tasking statements, which were placed in the bag. Here are the dowsing questions, expressed in general terms. (When you dowse a specific quatrain, the number of the quatrain is inserted into the question to make it more precise.)

1. "Does this prophecy accurately describe a present or future event?"
2. "Has the event that the prophecy describes occurred yet?"

In order for a quatrain to qualify for a scrying session, the answer to the first question had to be yes and the answer to the second one had to be no. Only the quatrains with this combination of dowsing results were represented in the grab bag.

For this screening process, I felt that dot matrix dowsing was my best choice as a dowsing technique because it is the least vulnerable to belief and expectation biases. Pendulum dowsing for these tasking questions could be done if the questions were obscured. If I were to do pendulum dowsing for the quatrains, I would screen several quatrains at once by placing the reference numbers of the quatrains on the front of index cards and the tasking questions on the back, then randomly draw a card and dowse it; or I would put tasking statements into the grab bag, then draw and dowse them one after another.

When I dowsed quatrain II.97, the first screening question dowsing went well and the response was acceptable to task the quatrain for scrying. The first question was "Does the prophecy of quatrain II.97 accurately describe a present or future event?" I dowsed a positive response—three quadrants with an even number of dots and one with an odd number of dots.

When I did the second screening question for dowsing on this quatrain, I ran into a problem. I had made a slight error when I initially worded the second question for the dowsing tasking. I want to share this with you so you can learn to avoid this mistake. I had been sloppy in my initial wording of the question. The original wording for the second question was "Is this prophecy of quatrain II.97 accurate?" The response was two boxes "yes" and two boxes "no"—a "no answer" response. After I dowsed the original version of question two for quatrain II.97, I had an intuitive feeling that the dowsing was off for some reason. Generally, if I get that feeling it means there is a problem with the tasking statement. This is something you can see in the dowsing results of the badly worded dowsing tasking question, and also feel. The feeling is that something is not right. This intuitive feeling is something that you develop with experience.

After rewording the second screening question, I made a second attempt at dowsing it. The wording of the tasking for the second attempt was "Has the event that quatrain II.97 describes occurred yet?" This question had a negative response. Of the four quadrants of the dot matrix square, three contained an odd number of dots. Only one had an even number, so the response was negative. Note that when you word the dowsing question for an individual quatrain, its title must be included in the question. Here my focus was on quatrain II.97. This focus has to be specific when you do the task.

When I make an error or have a "no response" answer, I am faced with two choices. I can look at my screening questions to see if they are vague or leading, or I can discard the quatrain and look for another one to screen. Most of the time if I get a nonspecific response, I discard the quatrain. This was a rare situation where I decided to repeat the dowsing of the questions. I reworded the second question for the second dowsing so it was more precise.

Whenever you do a second dowsing run on a question, the inquiry statement should always be reworded. This will help ensure accuracy of the dowsing. Wording your questions is very important when you dowse. Your accuracy depends on the statement being concrete and precise. My initial wording of the second question was too general, and there was a potential for error in the dowsing because of this poor wording. I corrected this in the second dowsing. I also tapped more dots on the second run, just in case I was encountering issues with belief bias. I had to make sure that I was not able to count the dots as I was working.

Case Study 1: Nostradamus, Century 2, Quatrain 97

The tasking statement drawn from the grab bag and set aside for the first case study was the tasking for quatrain II.97, the same quatrain that had given me trouble during dot matrix dowsing. This is the quatrain I had almost decided to discard.

> Roman Pontiff, take heed to come near
> To the City watered with two rivers,
> Thou shall spit there thy blood,
> Thou and thine, when the Rose shall blossom.
>
> *(Century 2, Quatrain 97)*

This first case study is the result of two sessions. I had difficulty with the first session, as I was fatigued prior to beginning it. I initially was going to discard the session. I did, however, save it, and the question was placed into the grab bag again. It was drawn a second time. This case study is a combination of the two separate sessions that relate to one quatrain (II.97). A question can be scryed more than one time. A second go-round with the subject will give more information about the inquiry. The repeating of the target resulted in different perspectives, so the two sessions present slightly different snapshots of the quatrain's data. When you scry a quatrain or prophecy, you are actually attempting to see the same thing the original visionary saw. You are essentially following the seer to the location and noting perceptions at that target site. Each time you do this, you will perceive a slightly different angle on that target.

These additional perspectives also occur when scrying a target in group scrying sessions. I observed an interesting phenomenon when a target was attempted by a group of seers: everyone had accurate aspects of the target present in their session, but all these aspects were different. It was almost as if they were communicating and coordinating telepathically so that there was no duplication. Yet all the different aspects were accurate and verifiable—the phenomenon was not due to inaccuracy.

Belief Bias Regarding Screening of Quatrain II.97

Though my feelings about quatrain II.97 were not particularly strong, I did carry some belief and expectation biases into this session. My belief bias was that this prophecy had not been fulfilled. It did not fit any of the known historical situations. The description of spitting blood indicates serious injury or death. There has been only one event of this sort since the time of Nostradamus: the assassination attempt of Pope John Paul II. The quatrain does not describe that event very well, so I did not think it was a fulfilled prophecy. I had to mentally isolate this belief while I dowsed the screening questions, and I realized that Nostradamus could have been looking into the past or into an alternative-reality timeline.

I also felt that because of the way quatrain II.97 is worded, there was an increased chance that it was an accurate prophecy. It is a description that contains a fair amount of detail even though it is very short. It captures an intense emotional ambience that was present during the vision. This was the belief and expectation I had going into the screening of the quatrain and the scrying session itself. I had to mentally isolate this belief and set it aside while I worked.

I mention how to deal with belief bias in session because even in a hidden target situation you can find yourself struggling with it. It is useful to understand the bias and be able to isolate it without regard to the level of conscious knowledge of the focus of the dowsing session. Stating and casting aside a belief or thought regarding a potential query before you begin the session is a good practice when you are working with questions that you might feel strongly about. To do this, you make a statement about what you expect from the session, then deliberately set that belief aside in a box or some other symbolic safe and solitary place. You can do this physically, by writing down your expectation and putting it into an actual box, or you can do it in your mind, by imagining these actions. This isolates the belief bias at least partially from the session and reduces the adverse influence of the belief on your perceptions.

First Scrying Session for Case Study 1

The tasking statement for this quatrain is "Go to the event described by Nostradamus in quatrain II.97 and describe the event, location, and entities he saw in that session." Here is a summary of the first scrying session. I did three primary information points and found *presence, object,* and *liquid*. The total time of the session was ten minutes.

The *presence* is moving up and down. There is an object near the presence that is cascading, has multiple vertical lines, and is hard, white, and cold. In the visual I see a bunch of horizontal lines that look structural. I would describe the appearance as being something similar to marble stairs. It has the same white, hard, stonelike appearance and feel to it. This is only a description of what the object looks like. The presence is interacting with this structural object through movement. The object also feels old and looks ancient. I have the label of "marble stairs" come up, and I break that label down into "white, hard, cascading, opaque," with a strong horizontal multiple-lined appearance.

At this time, I perceive *activity* going up and down this structural area, even though it is not on the first primary information list. This is interacting with the first aspect of primary information, which is the *presence*. The presence, the structural area, and activity are inseparable and interacting. The light and colors are strong and highly contrasting, some areas dark and others very bright. This is all around the aspect of the *presence*.

I then focus my scrying on the *object*, which is the second aspect of primary information. I perceive two long horizontal lines attached in the middle by a short vertical line. The object is metallic-looking and pointed on one end. The other end is brown and has a grainy appearance. At the time I scry it, I feel it is not a weapon per se but something else. In retrospect, I realize that I did not want to believe it was a weapon. It is a feeling of, "Oh no, it cannot be that." I feel a strong intention and focus. It is almost like I am trying to avoid something that is disturbing and upsetting to me. This kind of diversion can happen with emotionally intense situations encountered when scrying. I have had this happen a couple of times when asked to scry criminal activity or disasters. The object is an odd-looking thing, and I cannot identify if it was actually made as a weapon or is something that was improvised.

I move my focus to the third aspect of primary information, which is *liquid*. The liquid has a consistency like water and is translucent. It is contained in a chalice-like object, which is cupped and expensive-looking and encircles the water. Below this object containing the liquid aspect of primary information is an object that is structural and ladderlike in appearance. It is below the level of the liquid. This is noninteractive with the presence and the object, and appears isolated at the time of scrying.

The energy/activity related to the *presence* aspect that I perceive in session is the most important perception here, and it connects with me as I warm to the session. The event appears to happen with everyone involved on foot as opposed to in vehicles. There is intensity and intentional focus. Heightened emotions are present. This is an example of picking up an additional aspect of primary information during the session. In this case, the *activity* aspect seems to be more important than any other primary perception that I encountered initially. Expanding this session to explore the energy/activity and its relationship to the presence was a natural step. This perception of the activity also occurred in the second scrying session, in the same order.

Interpretation of the First Scrying Session for Case Study 1

The emotional intention and a sharp object were picked up. It had almost a ritual feel to it. It was in a public place and likely was in or near the sacristy of a church, with the chalice-like object being possibly the font at the entrance of the church or the baptismal font and oil stand where the sacramental oils are kept. None of the known papal assassination attempts fit the details I saw or the quatrain itself. Either the prophecy is inaccurate or it has not yet been fulfilled, or it was a priest or other clergy who was wearing something that made Nostradamus believe he was the pope. A mistaken identity by Nostradamus is the least likely option if it is a church setting. The traditional vestments of the pope were present and generally known in Nostradamus's time. I do not think the papal garb has changed much over the past four hundred years or so. I doubt he would be easily misled by modern garments.

After doing this scrying session on quatrain II.97 and opening the tasking statement for the feedback, I placed the tasking statement with quatrain II.97 back into the grab bag. This created the potential for drawing it again. When I drew the second tasking statement from the grab bag, I did a session without looking at the tasking statement until the end of the scrying session. Only after I revealed the task at the end of my scrying did I find that I had scryed quatrain II.97 again.

Second Scrying Session for Case Study 1

It was a fortunate occurrence to draw quatrain II.97 out of the grab bag a second time. In the second scrying session on quatrain II.97, I perceived more detail. The perceptions were also consistent with those of the first session.

The points of primary information to open the second session were *presence*, *object*, and *liquid*. In addition, I picked up *energy/activity* spontaneously during the scrying session. This happened much in the same way and at the same time as during the first scrying session, but it occurred earlier in the second session. It really seemed like I was trying to scry four aspects of primary information instead of three.

I examine the *presence* aspect of primary information first. I find the presence associated with the colors red and white. I perceive an associated structural object with a hard texture and an opaque clarity, which means the object is solid and light cannot pass through it. An image comes up that has a structural archlike appearance. The presence is located at the object and interacts with movement (*activity*). The associated structural object resembles the Arc de Triomphe in Paris in shape. It feels smaller than the Arc de Triomphe, however.

Continuing to scry, I perceive additional associated presences. They are related to the primary aspect of *presence*. The associated presence is dense and active, a large grouping of presences that are human, on foot, and densely packed. Despite the density, there is a uniformness to the secondary associated group of people. A number of those who are present are dressed in identical uniform-like objects. The objects and the multiple (crowd) presence perceptions are associated with the first primary aspect of a single *presence*. The crowd presence is a group of living beings that relate in some way to the single solitary presence.

I move to the *object* aspect of primary information. The appearance is the same lopsided, metallic, bladelike object that I perceived in the first session, with the metallic texture and color on one side and the grainy brown color on the other.

However, in this session, the object aspect does feel violent, harmful, and weapon-like. It is a really odd-looking object. It is not obvious, despite how the object feels, how it would be used. It seems more of a ceremonial piece in appearance than something someone would actually use as an assassin. It does not seem normal or straightforward in its purpose. There are conflicting perceptions with regard to its intended use. I continue to study the odd-looking object until my attention is drawn away from it by activity. At this point the session grows in emotional energy and intensity.

I perceive an inward movement toward a central area. The activity movement relates to the presences, both the singular presence and the group presence. It is inward-crushing and looks chaotic and dangerous. The intensity is such that I have to withdraw my attention from this perspective and shift to another one. I tend to do this when people are very angry or there is death. It is a natural protective mechanism that I have noted in my sessions that seems to prevent undue intensity of perception when I am working alone.

I pick up several significant objects present in addition to my previous perceptions. At this point the session is moving quickly, and staying organized and focused is a challenge. When this happens, I have to write very quickly and may not have time to label each aspect of primary information. I just write as quickly as I can, trying to catch all of the perceptions that come to me, and then sort it all out later.

I scry structural objects, and a label of "a cathedral" occurs. I break this label down into descriptive terms. The description is that it is "structural, historical, ritual-based, decorative, has metallic and stonelike features, and is old."

I pick up a transportation-related object that is scryed partially for an appearance of an oval with a dome on top, sort of like a flying saucer. The appearance is odd, and it is almost like one of the flying saucers seen in the cartoon *The Jetsons*—like a dome that is clear on top of another opaque metallic structure. It is on the ground and does not appear to be related to flight.

I move to the *liquid* aspect of primary information. There is an object that encircles water, is oblong and brown, smells metallic, and looks copperish or like old brass. This is possibly a fountain or pool, and it turned up in both sessions. In this session the water aspect has more of an appearance of a large structure and appears to be outdoors and not inside. There may be more than one significant container of water that is present at or near this event.

I then listen and I hear the following things: "I can hear them." "Run!" The voices sound angry. I feel the situation is escalating and dangerous. I hear explosions. I sense that more than one person is affected by this event. It feels widespread, as if it involves a city. This is related to the activity seen earlier of the crowd moving inward and the sense of danger and feeling of chaos.

Interpretation of the Second Scrying Session for Case Study 1

My interpretation of the feel of the location in the second scrying session is consistent with Western Europe. However, there are many areas in North America and Asia, particularly Western Asia, that have features that fit these scrying perceptions. I hear English and a European language being spoken—I believe it is French. It is spoken too fast for me to determine for sure. I can eliminate Spanish from the list of possibilities, because I speak Spanish well enough to recognize it even when spoken quickly and in the chaotic situation I found myself perceiving.

Even though this looks like France, and Nostradamus's prophecies are usually about France, it could be anywhere in the world. That being said, based on the quatrain and my own data, I think it could be Notre-Dame Cathedral. The Seine River splits, and the cathedral is on an island between the two branches of the Seine. This is consistent with the quatrain. I did not perceive a river during either scrying session, only the cathedral. The bodies of water that I picked up were significant but were also contained in associated structures. This is a large and important structure.

I did not get a clear image of the Roman pontiff spoken of in the quatrain. There were a number of people dressed alike, and he could have been any of them. As far as I could see, no one in this group had the appearance or presence of the current Pope (Pope Francis). This does not eliminate him, but it decreases the likelihood that he is a victim in this incident. Pope Francis also speaks Spanish as his first language. I would recognize his voice and language if I heard him speak or yell.

When you scry an event, you perceive snapshots of the action that is occurring. I may not have been looking in the right place. My attention was drawn to the area of activity and energy. It is also possible that if it was the current pope, he was not able to cry out or speak.

The violence is widespread and is directed at the entire population present at this location. It is very chaotic and hard to see exactly what happens. It is quite a large group of people.

The odd metallic object that seemed to be significant, and possibly a weapon, appeared in both sessions. It has an overall shape that is vaguely similar to a Nazi swastika missing an arm, or the runic *S* that the SS used during WWII. I cannot identify any sword or other weapon that has a similar appearance. It could be symbolic or represent a faction or paramilitary group.

The attack comes from outside and moves the crowd toward the center of the location. The number 37 appears in the session, but it is a disconnected perception and I do not have an interpretation for it. There is no context for it.

Based on the session data, it seems to be a summertime event. The air temperature felt pretty warm. Violence in large populations tends to happen more frequently in warm or hot weather than in the cold.

I do think that there were incidents leading up to this violent act. The event I scryed is an escalation of previous unrest. I do not think this is a targeted assassination. It is more like a generalized terrorist attack, military action against a gathered population, or a battle in a war. I would lean toward military action against a populace, as it is not a pinpoint or localized attack typical of terrorist actions, but rather an encircling by an aggressive group around a more passive group of people. Also, the people are not in military uniforms, but in religious garb. The initial ambience is one of ritual.

By examining the original tasking statement for the scrying session, I see which questions were answered. The original tasking was "Go to the event described by Nostradamus in quatrain II.97 and describe the event, location, and entities he saw in that session." The event was mostly described between the two sessions. The location was described adequately and the entities were described, but the specific entities of the pontiff and the assassin were not sketched or described.

Case Study 2: The First Temple of Solomon and the Ark of the Covenant

From a target pool of five hidden targets, which included such things as a living dinosaur, Stonehenge while it was being built, and the city of Atlantis, I drew the Indiana Jones target: the Ark of the Covenant, as it looked while it was housed in the legendary First Temple of King Solomon.

Accounts of this fascinating artifact occur mainly in the early books of the Old Testament and in Middle Eastern literature dating from about 500 BCE. The Ark of the Covenant was the holiest object of the nomadic Hebrew tribes under Moses, who for many generations housed it in a portable tabernacle—a kind of tent that could be folded up and carried when they had to move from place to place to graze their herds on fresh grass. After they crossed the River Jordan and established themselves in what became Judea, they were able to construct a permanent temple to hold the Ark, which took the place of the Tabernacle. King David received a vision of the Temple, but it fell to his son, King Solomon, to build it. This Temple is said in the Bible to have been located in Jerusalem, although no one today knows for sure what its actual location may have been.

The lore of Solomon's Temple is fascinating. It is related in a book titled the *Testament of Solomon*, which has been dated from the first century, although the story itself is much older. It is also referred to in the Babylonian Talmud. King Solomon was fabled to have been a great magician. God gifted him with the power of wisdom, and he used this wisdom to learn the magic of the ancient world. For occult reasons not specified in the Bible, the Temple had to be built without the sound of hammer, chisel, or any iron tool being heard in the Temple during its construction (1 Kings 6:7), a seemingly impossible requirement.

The Ark of the Covenant is the box constructed to hold the holiest objects possessed by the tribes of Israel while they wandered in the wilderness. Among these contents were the fragments of the two stone tablets inscribed by the finger of God with the Ten Commandments. The Ark was said to have been made of shittim wood sheathed in a layer of gold and surmounted by the images of two winged angels of the order of Cherubim, who faced each other. Between them is what is known as the Mercy Seat, where the actual living presence of God was supposed by the Israelites to manifest itself. So holy was the Ark that anyone who touched it, even by accident, was struck down as if by lightning.

First Scrying Session for Case Study 2

The tasking statement drawn from the grab bag and set aside unopened until after the session was worded as follows: "Scry the Temple and the Ark after the Temple had been completed and was in daily use during the reign of King Solomon."

When preparing the tasking statements for the grab bag prior to the scrying, I felt that there was enough supportive archaeological evidence for the existence of the Temple and King Solomon to go ahead with the scrying session. There was no need to do a preliminary dowsing of the tasking statement to verify its validity as a target, as was done with the statement concerning quatrain II.97.

The primary perceptions as I began this scrying session were *object*, *presence*, and *liquid*.

I move toward the object and scry a red and orange appearance. The object appears hot and glowing. A label of "fire" comes up and is broken down into the following: "It's for warmth and is something that draws people together." Fire is also representative of a destructive process. It is used in ritual. This fire has a ritualistic feel to it. It is related to sacrifice. It could be that the Ark of the Covenant is related to fire, or that the fire somehow represents the Ark symbolically.

The object that is glowing and red is located on top of a square blocky structure. There is a semicircle around this area that may represent a structure, possibly a cave, which is not what I was expecting (figure 6.1). The structure appears twice in the session and is either a building or a cave that has construction attached to it—I am not able to determine the orientation well enough to decide which of the two it is. I think the structure relates to the actual Temple, based on the sketch I did when I expanded the session. I do not think this is a large structure. It may be no bigger than a house. I do not think more than thirty people could fit in there comfortably. It would be tight even with that many.

Figure 6.1: A Cave-Like Structure

The second primary perception is *presence*. I have one presence who is center stage, as well as multiple other presences, a group about the size of an average classroom (thirty to fifty participants). The priestly presence relates to ritual sacrifice, and a label of "Temple" comes up.

The class-size group of presences are passive, receptive, and interested in what is happening. They are creating and enforcing community. The location has a cultlike atmosphere. They are also militant, sophisticated, and predatory. They have a life consistent with a herding culture, with some agriculture or gathering in season. The atmosphere is one of being entertained, but it feels somewhat sadistic to modern sensibilities. There is no empathy toward the prey. The group is insular, cohesive, and militant. It is not a pleasant place. I would not feel comfortable there.

There is a secondary presence who is the focus. He wears an odd-looking, tall hat (figure 6.2). I did not have any further perceptions of him other than his priestly role and his facial appearance. I receive the label of "temple," which is broken down and expanded.

Figure 6.2: Figure of a Priest

The third primary perception is *liquid*, and it relates to a larger body of water associated with transportation and food. Water does not seem to be an important primary perception, and it is deprioritized during the session. There also appear to be multiple shallow, creek-like bodies of water that have a bad taste, are greenish-brown, and relate to food. It looks like a delta-type water structure, with many branches off the main stream. It is flat and the water has a strong foul mineral taste.

I pick up the color white. I pick up a large white object, which is labeled "object 2" and will be branched later in the session. I feel that object 2 is the focus of the session.

Branching the Session

To do the branching, I drew a second square and assessed these three points of primary perception: *object 2*, *presence 2*, and *activity*. The number 2 indicates that this is the second primary perception of both *object* and *presence*. Since *activity* was not identified in the first set of primary perceptions, it does not need to have a number 2 following it. I continue with the internal scrying method as I continue to work through the target.

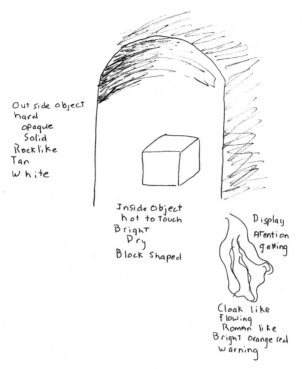

Outside object
hard
opaque
Solid
Rocklike
Tan
white

Inside Object
hot to touch
Bright
Dry
Block shaped

Display
Atention
getting

Cloak like
flowing
Roman like
Bright orange red
warning

Figure 6.3: Square Object beneath Dome

Object 2

I have a couple different objects associated with the primary perception *object 2*. The main focus of *object 2* is a square object in the center of a larger semidomed structure (figure 6.3). I am not certain that this dome shape is completely human-made. It feels like a natural feature of the landscape, like a cave. The shape and texture are very cave-like. The location seems to have been built up and structures added to it.

It is a hard structure with human-made aspects. It has a plain rocklike surface; it is white and not particularly large, maybe the size of a small modern farmhouse. My modest little house is about 1,500 square feet. I would say this structure is comparable in size, but a bit taller. It seems roomy inside. It has a semidome shape. The roof is rounded, but the walls are straight. It is taller than wide, longer than wide. The way the roof looks makes me think

I'm looking at a natural feature with added construction around it. It is predominantly white-colored, with some tan mixed in. It is cooler and more humid inside.

Inside the building-like object is the focus of *object 2*, which is a square structure. Based on the accounts of Solomon's Temple, I would say this is the Ark. It is blocky, bright, dry, hot, tan, and white, and a bright red cloth-like object is associated with it. There is not much to this structure. It does not look elaborate. I wonder why it feels so hot though. It feels warmer than it should. I wonder if there is a white rock-and-mortar casing around the object. I do not look inside. It feels spiritual, but no more so than any other spiritual object. I do not sense that I am about to be zapped by lightning or anything like that. In fact, it feels like I might not understand what I was looking at if I were to see this object and location.

The associated red object reminds me of a Roman cloak. It's about the same size as a cloak. It is a brilliant orange-red. It's a warning, attention-getting, flowing, and related to display. The interesting thing here is that it does not appear to be made of wool. It may be linen or cotton. The color is unusually bright. It has a great deal more orange than red to it. It does not look like the royal purple. I just use the term "cloak" as a comparison for the flowing nature of it. Could it be a glow of fire from the object seen in the first sketch? I am not sure. I do not think it is. The cloak-like object appears to be separate and physical. However, the sense of heat and the colors are the same as in the first perception, so it could be a fire around the artifact, or the artifact giving off some kind of radiation.

The box itself appears white and rather plain. It does not really fit the description of the Ark written in the Bible. The cloak-like object is near the boxlike object. It is not on it, and it is not covering it, as far as I can tell. Gold can be very red-orange in color, so if the color were covering the white boxy object, that would be more consistent with the biblical accounts of the artifact. When you are interpreting data like this, it is important to consider several possibilities and not just go with one that you might be biased toward.

The landscape reminds me of Central America or Mexico. There is a great deal of white, gray, and light tan. The climate is more tropical than I expected.

It is an odd combination of desert and tropics. It does not look anything like modern Israel. The creeks may be a delta, or water features that have since dried up. There are bluffs and a few small hills, but it is mostly flat land.

Figure 6.4: King Solomon

Presence 2

I will now examine *presence 2*. This presence is quite interesting. He is a very dark-skinned male (figure 6.4). The top of the head contains black and very curly hair. He has a beard but no moustache. He is physically strong, agile, small, lean, fit, and powerful, with a strong knowledge of the world, and spiritual. I believe this presence is either a priest or King Solomon. I picked up a priest earlier in the session when I scryed the first presence, so I'm inclined to think this is King Solomon himself. He has a different feel than the priest does—very militant, self-aware, and mentally sharp. Solomon was described as having a peaceful reign. I think that must be relative. We would not consider this man to be a peaceful ruler today.

Physically, he looks more African than modern Middle Eastern. He has a broad flat nose, high cheekbones, and extremely dark skin. He is well groomed. His hair is very coarse and curly, but it is more like the hair of a Middle Eastern man than someone of African descent.

Activity

Activity is related to ritual, sacrifice, fire, the animals, and the predatory activity of the humans gathered. This is more or less in harmony with a herding lifestyle. I have a strong sense of the ritualistic, cultish feel to this place and the way the animals are being killed. The people looking on are being entertained in a way that makes me feel very uncomfortable.

Session Summary for Case Study 2

I think the second session was a good one. I certainly did not expect the Temple to look like it did. The data in the session only loosely matched the biblical description. I think it is likely that King Solomon did exist and that the Temple and the Ark were actual physical objects. However, I do not think we would know what they were if we saw them. It's likely we have already found these objects and simply do not know their significance. The focus of the ritual activity seemed to involve killing animals, and that was disturbingly entertaining to the people who were involved as participants. The ritual activity has a cultlike, insular, ruthless, militant atmosphere that would be very objectionable to modern ideologies.

The location does not seem consistent with biblical accounts. Either there is perceptive error on my part or the landscape and climate have drastically changed since that time. It does not appear that the first Temple was built over by Herod's Temple. The site of the Herodian Temple is on a hill. This area was quite flat. If it was a cave, it was a very small one. In situations like this, where not all the aspects of the target are known, the feedback becomes a bit more difficult. I would have to do more research and generally keep an eye out for any artifacts found that are related to the First Temple. King Solomon allegedly had ties to Ethiopia. I would not be surprised if there were more family ties with North Africa before the Babylonian Captivity period than we are generally led to believe.

CHAPTER SEVEN
CASTING AND
ENVIRONMENTAL SCRYING

After you feel comfortable with internal scrying, you can start to work with scrying tools. Casting is an ancient method of divination that involves scattering or pouring a physical medium across a surface, then perceiving patterns and forms in the medium. Traditional kinds of casting include the practice of casting lots, cowrie shells, and the knuckle bones of sheep, which are used for divination by shamans. Some kinds of geomancy (earth divination) involve throwing dirt into the air and observing how it falls, or distinguishing patterns in arrangements of rocks. Dice, which today are used for gambling or gaming purposes, were originally a form of casting.

Casting is particularly helpful for those who have difficulty with traditional speculum scrying or are interested in casting as a divination tool. This technique is easier than speculum scrying. It is both a method of scrying in its own right and a stepping-stone to the use of a speculum. When you practice casting, you learn to use physical materials and your eyes to experience various aspects of the target. If you find that casting works for you, then you can use it alone or in combination with other methods. My goal in this book is to give you as many tools as you need for your scrying toolbox. Even if you are scrying spirits, you can use the casting method.

Some of the things you can use for casting are pebbles, crystals, bones, and shells, all of which will provide the scryer with the necessary visual information. For my work at home, I prefer to use multicolored uncooked rice as a portable medium, along with a hodgepodge of shells, glass, and pebbles I collect on the local beaches. I like working with complex abstract patterns, so I use a material that is fine, such as rice, as opposed to something coarse and large, like bones.

Even though rune casting is a traditional method of divination, it is not suitable for scrying. Scrying requires the mind to form and observe abstract patterns. It is not an oracular system, based on fixed definitions and meanings of the symbols. The casting method of scrying is a bit different from the traditional techniques of geomancy, astrology-based casting methods, and the Germanic runes. This method works by intuition alone and does not depend on formal symbols with specific meanings. Casting the medium onto a cloth with labels on it, such as astrological signs or geomantic divisions, is also not acceptable for this particular method.

Those needing to scry in a public place will find that casting cannot be easily done in total stealth. However, using small bags and fine, multicolored material will help you be more covert if you wish to work unnoticed. For stealth scrying, the most discreet method is to keep the casting material in a transparent ziplock bag. The material is moved around inside the bag to create patterns, then the bag is set on a table or other flat surface for study.

Learning and using the casting method of scrying is optional. If you are interested primarily in speculum scrying, you do not have to do this step if you do not want to. However, I have found when teaching scrying that some students need this extra step to make the transition from internal scrying to traditional scrying methods. Scrying patterns in the cast rice or other materials provides the required bridge to scrying in a crystal ball or mirror. Some practitioners will use casting as their preferred method of scrying, while others will move on to use the traditional speculums as well.

If you find this method of casting to be effective, it may be an indication that you would benefit from the use of a particular type of speculum when you progress to traditional scrying. The most common types of speculums are a clear crystal ball made of glass, acrylic, or rock crystal; a plain silvered mirror; or a basin of clear water. However, if you get good results with this casting method and find that you enjoy making out patterns, then you may experience better scrying success when you use a crystal ball that contains inclusions or water in a basin that has an irregular surface.

Tools for Casting

The casting method of scrying requires the use of a few simple household tools. You will need a bowl, cup, or cloth for casting the medium, and an airtight jar or container in which to store the dry uncooked rice. The bowl or cup should be wide and flattish. It doesn't matter what color it is, but it should not have any painting or engravings on the inside surface. A small plain cloth can also be used in place of a bowl, but care needs to be taken, as this can get messy. A clear ziplock bag might work better for situations where you do not want to risk spilling rice everywhere. If you prefer, you can use a teacup or coffee mug. Make sure it is clean and dry.

For portable casting, you will need colored rice. The three main natural colors of rice are brown, black, and red. If you can get all of these colors, that would be best. Otherwise, just use black and white. Mix equal quantities of all your colors. To add complexity to your casting patterns, you should break up some dried spaghetti into short pieces and mix it in with the rice. Also add in some lengths of black or white string, if you have some. Your purpose is to create a matrix in the rice that forms abstract and complex patterns.

Keep all these materials in a jar or other sealable container. Any old jar, such as an olive jar or a small jam jar, will do, provided it is clean and dry. I would sprinkle some dried herbs in there as well to keep the jar from developing an unpleasant odor. If you are working under time and place constraints, then the jar, cup, or bowl into which you cast the material should be small. A ziplock bag to carry these materials is a convenient substitute for a jar. Keeping rice in a cloth bag does not work well—you need a container with an air-tight seal. Rice tends to get everywhere and is messy if you use only a cloth bag.

When you cast, you are looking for shapes, lines, and other basic visual information about the target. This is a completely different approach from older methods of casting, which rely on specific fixed meanings for cast items and their patterns. This method uses your intuition. There are no book meanings to memorize concerning the shapes and forms seen in the rice or other media. With traditional methods, there are set meanings to the patterns formed by the casting medium. Good examples of this are tea leaf reading and coffee ground reading. There is usually a fixed symbology that is based on shapes and their resemblance to objects, and a set of meanings that are arbitrarily or traditionally associated with those appearances.

By using the casting method of scrying, you will learn to work strictly from intuition. If you see a pattern, even if it looks like an object that you know, it should be handled in the same way you deal with a label when doing internal scrying. That is to say, the label should be written out, and then a description of the scryed visual aspects of the label should be written below it. The outline of the shape should be sketched as well. As you work with this process, you will find that the descriptions and sketches contain more pertinent information about the point of primary information (and the target) than the label does. As that happens, it becomes much more natural to break down the label and to focus on the descriptive information and the outline sketch.

In other words, if you see something—say, a horse or a tree—it does not have inherent meaning. In traditional casting, a horse might mean travel, or a tree, stability. In this method, you do not consider any equivalencies or correspondences at all. You are looking only for basic shapes and lines. Also, you are casting and reading the primary information aspects and not the actual target, because you are working with a hidden target, just as you do with internal scrying.

So if you see something that looks like a horse, consider the horse to be a label. Break it down by describing aspects of the horse. In this example, a horse might be broken down into "black, running, fast, moving." The activity "running, fast, moving" is another primary information point, and needs to be set aside and examined after you finish the original three primary information points that you put into a square at the beginning of the session. I would also draw an outline of the outer edge of the horse. That shape is likely to show up when you look at your feedback.

Procedure for the Casting Method of Scrying

1. The setup of the session for this method is the same as the one described in the first chapter. The inquiry needs to be broken up into various related questions, or several different inquiries need to be placed in a grab bag. Both approaches are designed to conceal the specific question you are scrying. The slip of paper stating the task needs to be taken out and set aside without being looked at.

2. Identify your three points of primary information. This is the same procedure I wrote about in the second chapter of this book.

3. Dump your mixture of rice into a bowl. (Add pieces of spaghetti and string if you wish.) Initially, before you begin to scry, you can play with it, stir it with your fingers, etc. Then gaze into the rice and look for shapes that grab your attention and that you feel are related to the visual aspects of the point of primary information that you are working on. You are basically connecting the dots in the rice. You will be looking mainly for shapes, but other things will come to mind related to color, texture, position, purpose, and lighting. These need to be written down as they are brought into your awareness. You want to move quickly, without feeling overly rushed. This procedure should be worked within the span of a few minutes. Stir the media at intervals as you work so that new shapes and patterns are formed in the casting material. Interaction with the casting material is important. It is desirable to touch and physically move it around.

4. Shapes that remind you of specific objects, such as a house or a tree, are labels. These labels should be broken down in the same way we just discussed. You ask yourself, "How does this (label) remind me of the point of primary information that I am exploring?" Then write down your response as quickly as possible. Your focus is on describing the primary information points and not on attempting to guess what is at the location.

5. I recommend doing three points of primary information for a session of fifteen minutes. You can do another primary information box if you have more time. You can also do multiple sessions for one inquiry.

The visual information you gather from casting will be quite simple in nature. The shapes, colors, and sometimes spatial relationships are the data that you see in the rice. The rest of the information regarding the primary information point will come to you intuitively, much as it does during internal scrying.

Environmental Scrying

Environmental scrying involves scrying your physical surroundings for shapes and patterns. It is similar to casting in that you are looking for visual patterns that you intuitively feel are related to points of primary perception. Environmental scrying is best used in outdoor settings. It can be done indoors, but it is more difficult. For a beginner, it is easier to start with an exterior location. I will go over two basic methods of environmental scrying. The first is used in combination with field dowsing, and the second is used with a target that is taken out of a grab bag.

Method One of Environmental Scrying

When you are field dowsing, you can train yourself to scry for the target. Narrow the area by dowsing, then work on seeing a slight shimmer above the target. It looks like a heat shimmer seen more in the peripheral vision. A heat shimmer appears in the air when the hot sun shines on a dark surface. It looks like a distortion of the vision. When you scry, look for something that resembles that kind of distortion but not as strong, and that disappears when you look directly at it. Soften the focus of your eyes and keep your gaze steady as you cover that area. The shimmer is usually not far above the target—less than a foot most of the time. It appears fairly quickly and is not consistent. It comes and goes. You do not want to scry a large area at a time, but rather to do a systematic search, scrying small chunks of territory as you work through a location.

To learn environmental scrying, practice with a known object that you can easily find, such as a coin, stick, small knickknack, or toy. Toss it in the grass in a small area to be searched, and scry for the shimmer above it. Once you have an idea of what the phenomenon looks like, you can work with things that are buried or placed where you have to do some hunting.

The shimmer is quite subtle. It is not nearly as powerful in appearance as an actual heat shimmer. It is best to do this with the sun at a lower angle— dawn and twilight are the best times. If you only have a few minutes to practice at lunchtime, you can still do it, but it may take a bit more effort to see the tell-tale shimmer than it would if you learned this technique with the sun at a more ideal angle. If you live in northern latitudes, the sun does not climb to a high angle in the sky between November and mid-February, so you can work any time during that period. The same holds true for Australia and other lands in the Southern Hemisphere between May and July.

I practice this method with pennies in the grass. I have a fairly small area that I work in. We have a variety of terrain on our property, so I can also work in woods and on the beach, as well as in a pasture. I throw the penny down and then try to scry above it to see this shimmering effect. If I lose the penny, which does happen sometimes, it is not of any concern. Beaches are a great place to practice dowsing, and I have found a few interesting "treasures"—items not of any particular monetary value but interesting. Spent eighteenth- and nineteenth-century rifle slugs, or replicas thereof, are one example of curiosities I have located with this art.

Method Two of Environmental Scrying

The second method of environmental scrying is to use the environment as you would the bag of casting material. You look at the natural features in the landscape and allow your mind to perceive shapes and patterns. If you are in a situation where you prefer your scrying not to be noticed, this is a good method to work with. You "stir" the medium by moving around physically, going to slightly different locations to give yourself fresh perspectives.

I recommend using a voice recorder and determining the points of primary information prior to going outside, by using the grab bag to select a hidden target and then setting down three points within a square to scry.

Once the points are determined, you can memorize them for the session and record your scrying data concerning those points on the voice recorder. This looks a bit less conspicuous than running around staring at trees and grass while writing on a clipboard. You scry the environmental features, such as the shapes of tree limbs, masses of leaves, plants, and buildings, for patterns that draw your attention as being related to the aspect of primary information that you are working on.

You can usually do three primary information points in a fifteen-minute session. Once you have completed the scrying session, make sure to transcribe your voice recording onto paper, and do your sketches at the same time that you do the transcription. The feedback session after you reveal your hidden target is important as well. If you walk while you are doing this environmental scrying technique, it will provide a changing matrix that is much like stirring up the casting media.

Any time you are doing casting or environmental scrying using this second technique, you are working with the square containing three points and the primary information that is perceived at those points. The target is hidden and drawn from a grab bag. This should be done regardless of the type of divination technique you are using. The first technique of environmental scrying is a bit different. With that, you are working with either a semi-hidden target—a penny in the grass, for example—that you cannot see with a casual glance or a buried target that you cannot see at all unless you dig for it.

Casting Method of Scrying Case Study

I set up four targets for the grab bag:

1. The exterior and interior of the Great Pyramid at Giza at 11:00 a.m. on May 3, 2019.

2. The Newfoundland ferry terminal at North Sydney, Nova Scotia, on December 10, 2019, at 8:00 a.m.

3. The interior of the Smithsonian Museum of Natural History in Washington, DC, on December 10, 2019, at 10:00 a.m.

4. The ruins of Tintagel Castle in Cornwall on July 5, 2019, at 1:00 p.m.

Tasking statements are written for each target. All times of day are local time at the sites of the targets. The tasking statements are placed in a grab bag for a random draw to assign the session a hidden target. I have my casting materials ready. In this case, they consist of a collection of rocks, twigs, and other natural materials that I had collected over the years. I decided to work with my mix of oddities this time instead of rice.

On my paper, I create my square and make my three dots representing the points of primary perception. The first point of primary perception is *object*, the second is *activity*, and the third is *presence*. As I create my square, I perceive a feeling of dryness and difficulty in breathing.

The first primary perception of *object* gives an impression of a right angle, an acute triangle, a cube shape, the colors gray and tan, and a sense of bigness. This sense of bigness is not seen in the media, but rather my attention is drawn to the largest items present in the media, and it feels big. It also feels immobile.

The second primary perception is *activity*. I am attracted to the fine grains in the medium and receive an impression of something fine or refined. The description "liquid, gray, slate stone" grabs my attention. "Shale" is a label that I perceive, and it breaks down to "oily and black-colored, with an acrid smell."

The third primary perception is *presence*. I see a few grains off to the side. The grains seem less numerous there than in other areas. The grains are protected, dark. There should be more presence than there is at this time.

This is the session data—now I look to see what my target is. I discover that it is number two: the Newfoundland ferry terminal in North Sydney, Nova Scotia. At the date and time in the target statement, there was a raging rainstorm with hurricane-force winds. The ferry boats were moored in their slips, and no trips to Newfoundland were made on that day. There are three ferries that take passengers, cars, and supplies to and from Newfoundland. Each ferry is big enough to hold a few hundred people, cars, and trucks. They are solid, seaworthy vessels that often have to cross dangerous, rough waters.

Session Data

In this session, the first point of primary perception, *object*, is the main focus of the target. The Newfoundland ferry boats are white and gray. The angle of the sketch I made looks much like the bow of the boats. It is an acute angle and a cube shape. The visual data I received consisted of this angle and a boxy shape. The boats are sturdy and broad and are designed to hold and carry a large amount of cargo—they are boxy. The gray color I was attracted to in the casting media is identical to the gray on the ships.

On the date in the tasking statement, there was a rainstorm with strong winds, typical of this area in late fall. The winds were near hurricane strength, and the boats had to be slipped and moored to prevent damage or capsizing in the heavy seas. They could not leave the harbor. The perception of immobility occurred because they were not able to be moved. This perception was felt but not seen in the casting media. This provides a good example of how this kind of scrying works. You will feel things as you see them in the casting media. The idea of immobility characterized conditions at the primary target. Everything was shut down. Nothing could move until the wind settled down.

The second point of primary perception is *activity*. The fuel used on the Newfoundland ferries is a heavy diesel oil. The fuel is related to the motion of the boat but is not the major activity occurring at the site. This is not the most accurate perception. Even though it is present at the location, there is a discrepancy between the primary perception and the data from the casting.

The third perception is *presence*, and the major aspect of this was that there was less of it than usual. This was represented by isolated grains of sand that attracted my attention in the casting media. At the ferry terminal, the usual crews and passengers were not present on December 10, 2019. The only people present were the boat crew needed to keep the boats from being damaged during the storm. There might have been some office workers in the terminal as well, but there were fewer people than normal, and those who were working were protected inside the ferries' wheelhouses or in the office facility at the terminal.

Analysis of Feedback

The data for *activity*, even though it is describing something that is present and related to the motion of the boats, is not as good as it should be, and I would consider that a miss. The motion could be related to the motion of the boats at their moorings and in the slips, as well as the activity of the few people working there. Instead, I picked up the liquid that fuels the boats. It is possible that they were fueling while I did the session, as they often do that in the mornings. There is a distinctive and very foul smell to boat fuel, which I recognized right away when I worked that point of perception; however, it should have been a *liquid* perception, since that is a primary feature of this target. Everything else I would consider to be a hit. The perceptions of immobility and fewer presences than normal are particularly pertinent to the conditions present on the day and time of the tasking.

For a beginner, I would not be so harsh in my evaluation. When you are starting out and just getting your feet on the ground with this skill, and you get something like that for the *activity* aspect of the primary perception, I would consider that a hit. Even as an advanced practitioner, it is always important to look for places where you can improve accuracy. This is a good example of a concrete target where skills can be improved and perceptions sharpened. Details are important when you are doing feedback.

CHAPTER EIGHT
SCRYING TAROT

O f all the skills that I cover in this book, scrying Tarot cards is my favorite. I enjoy working with the cards in session, and I find that my results
are sometimes spectacular when I use the Tarot as part of my overall scrying
session. In my personal scrying practice, I use a combination of techniques.
Some of the Tarot techniques that I use are covered in this chapter.

Scrying Tarot cards is a completely separate technique from reading them
as oracles, which is the usual way the cards are read. The oracular interpretation of the cards relies on the fixed, established esoteric meanings of the
cards as the primary source of information, and the way that information is
paired with a particular situation or prediction.

In the method of scrying the Tarot that is described in this book, you
will be looking at the cards in a different way. Your scrying data is obtained
from the various shapes, lines, colors, and other visual aspects of the cards as
well as the visual feel of the cards rather than from a study of the divinatory
meanings of the cards. Tarot scrying relies entirely on an intuitive glance at
the visual characteristics of the Tarot card. It does not matter which card is
drawn.

For those who are experienced in doing Tarot readings using traditional
oracular methods, think of this not as a criticism of those methods but as an
additional tool for your divination tool kit. I do not want to give the impression that I believe scrying a deck is better than oracular interpretation. Both

have their place as divination tools. I do want to make a distinction between the two, and to explain how to scry the cards as an additional or alternative use to oracular reading.

The Tarot scrying method I am teaching here works better and more accurately for space-time targets than the oracular method does. It is excellent for targets that do not directly involve people, such as archaeological artifacts, climate targets, and space or sea exploration. Traditional methods of interpreting the Tarot do not lend themselves well to these purposes, and if the oracular meaning is used in this manner, the reading may lack data and accuracy. The method provided here will help address some of those challenges of using the cards for nontraditional subjects such as physical targets and events.

Using Tarot scrying will help you as an oracular Tarot reader as well as give you a powerful, convenient scrying technique. Oracular Tarot works best when dealing with internal mental and spiritual conditions, channeling spirits, and gaining insight into challenges related to personal growth. If you use both techniques for their appropriate purposes, you will have a potent tool for divination work.

When you scry the Tarot, you allow the data you are seeking related to the points of primary information to arise spontaneously from the abstract visual patterns on the cards and the way the card patterns interact with each other. It is identical to casting. You are looking for shapes, colors, and textures. Allow the shapes, lines, colors, and other visual aspects of the cards to grab your attention. Only some, but not all, of the aspects of the Tarot card you are scrying will attract your notice. When this happens, you record the specific shapes, lines, colors, and energy patterns that come to you while you are observing the cards. These observations of the aspects of the cards that you feel relate to the aspects of primary information you are working with form the data of your scrying session. As with casting and internal scrying, preference should be given to sketching the information whenever it is possible.

Characteristics of a Scrying Tarot Deck

I have found that certain types of Tarot decks work better for scrying. In the course of my personal practice, I have discovered that the main qualification for a scryable deck is that it should have abstract or surreal artwork. This kind of artwork does not necessarily depict a scene that is identifiable, or that tells a story, or that looks like the scene of a play. The images should hint at the meaning of the card but contain complex visuals, often in layers and in unexpected proportions and colors.

An abstract image does not contain identifiable objects. You need to use your imagination to complete the object. A surreal image has an unnatural combination of objects that usually don't go together. An example of this is Hans Ruedi Giger's art, which combines alien machines with familiar organic and sexual components. He is the artist who designed the look for the *Alien* series of movies, and is probably one of the best known exponents of modern surrealism.

The only deck I have that is sort of an exception to the abstract-surreal art rule is the miniature deck I use when I have to work in limited space. It is a Rider-Waite deck that I picked up in the late 1990s. There are only a few miniature Tarot decks available that are suitable for scrying. This one does not have captions, so I use it when the situation calls for it.

The Thoth Tarot contains both abstract and surreal artwork and is one of the best decks for doing scrying. The only disadvantage to it is that modern versions of this deck have the oracular meanings captioned at the bottom of the cards. This is an unfortunate trend in published Tarot cards and creates additional obstacles for scrying. I prefer decks that do not bear card captions spelling out the divinatory meanings of the cards. I find that these meanings can be a distraction, and I do not refer to them when Tarot scrying. However, it is becoming increasingly rare that decks are published without the card meaning spelled out on each card, so if you like a deck and it has good abstract artwork, you may be able to learn to ignore the written meanings on the cards.

The deck of cards you use does not have to be perfect. You can mix incomplete decks or use decks that are flawed in some way. You can use more than one deck at a time for the session if you want to. You can also mix the cards with casting materials, and use both the front and the back of the cards. Combining your old incomplete decks with casting materials is a good way to make use of incomplete or flawed Tarot decks.

The problem with having the oracular meaning written on the bottom of the card is that it will lead the scryer into storytelling or labeling. We have covered labeling already. The written meaning may throw some scryers right into that trap. Storytelling is the other trap you need to avoid. That is where you start to develop a story line about the points of primary information. The feeling of putting it all together is the sense of the storytelling trap. This is a function of the analytical mind and should be avoided. If you find yourself spinning a story line, you have lost contact with your deeper mind.

The captioned oracular meanings of the cards will tend to throw you right into the storytelling trap and derail your connection to the deeper mind. This will prove more challenging for experienced Tarot readers, especially those who know the accepted traditional meanings of the cards by heart and who were taught to spin a story using the cards when doing readings. Storytelling has entertainment value and makes the reading more interesting, but it is a trap that leads to inaccuracies in scrying work, especially when doing highly specific physically based targets.

Usually you will have to make a compromise. The most abstract Tarot decks readily available are captioned. As a scryer, you need to either use a marker to black out the meanings or learn to ignore them. I prefer the latter way, as I like to keep my decks as pristine as possible. Another option is to purchase a deck from a foreign country. I have a Russian and a Chinese Tarot deck. I cannot read either language, so even though they are captioned, the captions have no meaning to me.

Two of my favorite decks are the Hermetic Tarot and the Thoth Tarot. I like to use both decks for scrying, but unfortunately they have an oracular caption at the bottom of each card, so rather than discard the decks entirely, I have just learned to ignore the captions. As an experienced Tarot reader, I had the meanings for most of the cards in various decks memorized when I started to change my technique from reading the oracular meanings of the cards to scrying them. I had to overcome the tendency to favor the oracular meanings.

Rigorous feedback is the key to getting out of the storytelling trap. There is a tendency among Tarot readers, including myself, to waffle on feedback, because they want to be accurate and they have a natural fear of "getting it wrong." You must look honestly at your results by using predictions that are completely black-and-white. Examples of straightforward predictions are gaming predictions and market-value predictions for a specific day or time period. You track your "hit" percentage versus your "miss" percentage. After a few major misses, usually ones that you were absolutely sure you got right, you will loosen your mental hold on the oracular meanings of the cards. Challenging yourself with that kind of prediction using Tarot cards also helps you get over your fear of failure. You will miss fairly frequently doing this. The percentage of hits will increase slowly when you work with inflexible, straightforward targets.

Beginner Tarot Scrying

As a beginner, you are advised to completely ignore the oracular meanings and go only with the shapes, lines, and actions that appear on the cards that you feel are related to the points of primary information. If you find that you are getting into a story line or scrying inaccurately, it means that you are allowing labels to slip into your work. When you buy a Tarot deck for scrying, put the accompanying instruction booklet in a safe place and leave it there. The accepted traditional meanings for the cards are not going to help you scry.

If you find that you are struggling with accuracy, you can try changing decks. Always make sure you are scrying the aspects of primary information that you divined at the beginning of the session. The target is hidden, and you are focused on those points and nothing else. Do not get frustrated if the first few sessions are off. Keep at it. Consistently follow the structure of the session using the grab bag technique and the three points of primary information explained in chapter 2. As you get used to the structure and technique and more skilled at setting aside the labels and story lines, you will experience more confidence and greater accuracy in your work.

Focus on describing the points of primary information: *object, liquid, presence,* and *activity/energy.* Scenes depicted on the cards will not tell you about the inquiry. Instead, allow your eyes to be drawn to shapes, textures, and other visual information that will help you describe the aspects of primary information.

One advantage of using Tarot for scrying is that it is a good system when you need to work a quick session. I find the Tarot easier to work with than casting. It is less messy and, once you get the hang of it, very accurate. A miniature deck is handy for doing scrying. Miniature decks are readily available and easy to carry if you want something small and unobtrusive that takes up a minimum amount of space on the table.

I know that many practitioners want to do rituals of cleansing and consecration with their Tarot cards. I am not one of these. I have worked with decks that were consecrated and decks that I just took out of the box, shuffled, and used. I have not found any difference between the two. I have found that the deck I sketched by hand seems to work a little bit better for me, but those cards are large and not very practical to use in public settings. I also use decks that I purchased or that came to me by other means, but I have not done anything special with those decks as far as cleansing and consecration are concerned. Up to this point I have not had any problems with them. If I did have a problem with a deck, I would address it by changing the deck. Depending on my mood, I may arbitrarily switch around and use different decks. I sometimes use more than one deck in a session.

Tarot Scrying Method

Step 1. You will be using the hidden target grab bag. The setup for this session is identical to that for casting and internal scrying. Identify three points of primary information in the same way you learned for other types of scrying. You do not draw the cards to identify the primary information points. The session begins exactly as it does for internal scrying and casting. This is always the case whether you are casting, using Tarot, or using a traditional speculum.

For each point of primary information, I usually draw three cards after shuffling the deck. This is not a hard-and-fast rule. I would suggest drawing only two or three cards to start with. The number of cards you draw is not of great importance. I'm giving you this number only because two to three cards are convenient and compact. They give a good variety of visual information without overstimulation. The layout of the cards is a consideration with this method. You can hold them or set them down, whatever is most convenient. I set the cards down so I can study them easily and sketch what I see.

Step 2. After you have identified three points of primary information, work with one point at a time. Study the cards you have drawn, looking for shapes, colors, and textures. Write down what catches your eye first. Write it down quickly. Do not stop and think about it too much. Jot down a few shapes, textures, colors, and the emotional ambience, then move on. If you feel that you want to pull more cards after looking at three cards on a primary information point, go ahead and do it.

Remember, you are still exploring one aspect of primary information at a time. The colors, shapes, textures, and other information you perceive intuitively relate to the primary information points. You are not trying to guess the target. Labels that turn up are handled and broken down the same way as for internal scrying or casting. Draw additional cards if you feel you want more information about the point of primary information you are working on. The number of cards you use is up to you. It is done entirely by intuition.

Step 3. If additional primary information aspects turn up while you are scrying the cards, set these points aside, finish the current point, and then move to the next one in the box. The new primary information points that are set aside should be addressed after you finish working with the box you are on. Do not skip around to different boxes. This will help you stay organized and orderly.

If for some reason you need to backtrack and you decide before the target is revealed that you want more data on a particular point, then you can go back to that point at any time, even if a significant amount of time has elapsed.

Repeating a target is not detrimental to your work or well-being. I find that I get more and better information on the second or third round with a particular target, and oftentimes after scrying a target, I will put it back in my grab bag. It does not matter how much time has elapsed. I have done some targets years apart and the results are consistent.

Step 4. Sketch your perceptions as much as possible. There is no question in my mind that this is the best way to record information obtained in a scrying session. Refer to chapter 3 for directions on sketching. It is important to understand that when you sketch from a Tarot deck, you are only outlining shapes that you feel have similarities to the primary information. Maintain the rules regarding labeling and guessing. The cards will not show what the target is. You will only be able to find similarities in general shapes and atmosphere to the inquiry.

Nonvisual Data

Once mastery of the incoming nonphysical visual data is attained, then explorations of other sensory information can be done. As you advance with the Tarot scrying technique, you will find that other nonphysical senses come into play when looking at the cards. You will hear something or sense something in the energies and atmosphere of the primary information. You may smell or taste things as well.

When you detect something in the energies and atmosphere of the card, occasionally the card's esoteric meaning will match what you sense. If this happens, then and only then can there be a relationship between the primary information and the oracular definition of the card. Even if you are advanced, you may find that the esoteric definition of the card throws you into a labeling trap. If this happens, discard the canned card information.

As a beginner, I suggest that you focus on the visual aspects of the cards and the points of primary information. Scrying is first and foremost visual information as it relates to the primary information aspects you are exploring. It is important to learn to identify descriptions of the primary information points through the imagery of the cards. If the meaning of a card is used as the main means to relate to the primary information, it will result in a labeling trap and inaccurate data.

When you do feedback and interpret your data by comparing it with the tasking statement, you can sometimes figure out the story behind the target. The following case study is a good example of this. The data itself did not reveal much, but when I compared the cards to the tasking statement and incorporated more of the esoteric meanings of the cards when I interpreted the raw data, it yielded some very interesting things. Even though this is not the best case study for a beginner target, it was an interesting experience, and I thought it would be a good one to share with you. Several aspects were perceived in a very visceral way. There are also interesting interpretation aspects that beginners and advanced scryers alike need to be aware of when they are looking at their scrying data during the feedback session.

Tarot Scrying Case Study

For this case study, I used the Llewellyn Tarot deck. It does have scenes on it and is not as abstract as some decks, but it also has complexity and good color that I find helpful. The deck I used is missing a couple of cards due to critter damage. However, it is still useful for this purpose.

The following four targets were placed in the grab bag:

1. The inside of the British Museum, the John Dee exhibit, on December 10, 2019, at 2:00 p.m.
2. Tutankhamun's tomb after opening it and the first look inside by Howard Carter on November 4, 1922.
3. The Eiffel Tower on December 10, 2019, at 2:00 p.m.
4. Dr. John Dee's Mortlake residence on March 10, 1582, at 11:00 a.m. (which is the date of the entry in John Dee's diaries when he first met Edward Kelley—see page 66 of *Five Books of Mystery*, edited by Joseph Peterson).

All times are local time at the locations of the targets. Tasking statements were made for the four targets and placed in the grab bag. One was chosen. The chosen target was number three: the Eiffel Tower on December 10, 2019, at 2:00 p.m. It was set aside without being opened and identified. The struggle I had with this scrying was that I really wanted the fourth target to be the one I drew, so I was fighting perceptions with a fantasy. In the end I had some spot-on perceptions, but also some that were inaccurate.

I drew my square box and placed in it three dots representing three points of primary perception. The first point was *presence*, the second point was *object*, and the third point was *presence*.

The first point of primary information was *presence*. The cards drawn were the Priestess and the Ten of Cups.

I had a sense that there were multiple presences doing random things, and that they somehow had the greater benefit—they were inside, and that seemed to be more profitable and pleasant. I perceived a doorway that was rounded on top and smooth—an inverted U shape. It seemed to be dark inside the tower. I also picked up that this was a long, thin, tall object. My focus went to the object immediately, almost before I was really ready to do the perception.

The *object* was the second point of primary perception. The cards scryed were the Tower and the Page of Pentacles.

The object had a special entrance that seemed to separate those with special benefit from those who did not have special benefit. Descriptions of the object were spot-on. I perceived something tall and slender, a tower, not just regarding the identity of one of the cards drawn but as significant to the details of the shape of the object. I had gray and black as the colors. I had a lacy appearance to it. The presence on the outside seemed to be related to dejection, lack of benefit. I drew on my paper a tower shape that was layered and lacy. The sketch was really on target.

The third point of primary perception was *presence*. The cards used were the Eight of Cups and the Queen of Pentacles.

This presence seemed to be on the outside, and seemed to be somewhat sad or distressed. This was a single presence that I focused in on. It is possible that this was a person present there at the scene who was reaching out to my deeper mind, perhaps sensing my study of the target. In situations like this, I have no way of verifying this presence. Someone who is emotionally upset may grab your attention for a few minutes. This may be a search for comfort and for someone who will empathize with their situation.

This, however, is speculation. I have no way of verifying or negating this presence outside of the structure. So technically it would be classified as an unknown. I would not classify this as a miss, because there is a fair chance that this does describe someone who was outside of the tower structure. People were walking outside of the structure at that time. As a beginner, you want to try to minimize the use of targets that can't be verified and create this kind of speculative data in session. However, you are almost certain to encounter at least some unknown information about any given target, regardless of how well known your target is.

Conclusion

I normally recommend that three cards be drawn at a time, but there seemed to be enough data in the two cards I drew to use for the session. The session took about fifteen minutes. The deck I used is not one I normally use for scrying. I chose to work with this unfamiliar deck because it helped replicate for me some of the issues that are faced by a beginner scryer, by introducing an unfamiliar component into the session.

I cannot dismiss the presence I sensed on the outside of the tower as being without validity. It may have been someone outside the tower at that time who was homeless or who had something bad happen to them. This is a possibility, but is an unverifiable perception that I cannot really do much with. In general, the object perceptions were quite well focused, and overall I feel good about the results of this session.

As with casting, Tarot can be used as a stand-alone scrying method or it can be a training tool for speculum scrying, which will be covered in the next chapter. Using more than one scrying method in a session can provide the scryer with additional data. You will find that you are stronger in one method than another, and will eventually find yourself using a couple of different methods based on your strengths and the type of information you need to get out of the session.

CHAPTER NINE
SCRYING WITH SPECULUMS

A speculum is a traditional scrying tool. The idea behind speculum scrying is to induce visions using a blank screen. This visual screen has specific characteristics and can be made from a variety of materials. The vision induced by the scryer comes from an internal source. It is not caused by the speculum.

Speculum scrying works by creating a channel from the deeper mind and programming it to link to the part of the brain that relates to vision. The information comes from the deeper mind, and you train your mind to process the information in a visual format. The speculum is used like a computer screen. The scryer's focus is trained to produce the vision on the chosen type of speculum.

Before we had movies and photographs, the closest thing that resembled these now familiar forms of media were reflections seen in water, clear crystals, mirrors, and certain metals such as mercury and electrum. The process originally used in scrying was to create a reflection in the mirror of a different place. Reflections were already known to be illusionary, so the illusion was mentally changed to reflect a location, person, or event other than what was present in the immediate environment. It had to be a reflective surface to create this effect. A modern equivalent to this would be the screen of a television, phone, or computer monitor. These items reflect a place other than where the viewer is. The idea is that the mind creates the illusion by transmitting the information from the deeper mind to the screen.

If you are wondering where I got this explanation, it was given to me by seers who lived a couple of centuries ago and are also familiar with the modern world. They now work as ancestral spirits, helping their descendants and others who express an interest in them. I did not even consider the mechanism behind the choice of speculum other than that it was traditional. This understanding should make it a little easier for people to work with speculum scrying. Just as spirit voices are slight changes in sounds that already exist in the environment, the scryed vision is a slight change in the environmental reflection found on a reflective surface.

A secondary technique related to speculum scrying is eyelid scrying. This again has a similar mechanism of action. The natural visuals show slight changes that reflect the deeper mind. It is done through mental training and adapting a natural physiological phenomenon to give information from the source of all information, the deeper mind. Eyelid scrying is discussed in detail toward the end of this chapter.

With most of us, scrying ability has to be developed. A few people experience naturally intense visions when they gaze into a reflective surface or close their eyes. For these individuals, the mental process of scrying is learned very early on in their lives, and it sometimes develops a frightening intensity. There is no advantage to increased visual intensity when scrying. A person trained in and working with proper technique will have accurate sessions regardless of their experience with speculum scrying. My goal in this book is to teach you how to accurately scry, not to develop intensity of your visions. Intensity may or may not increase with practice. The object is to learn what works for you regardless of the type of vision you experience, and then to develop those scrying skills to pinpoint accuracy.

Characteristics of a Scrying Speculum

Several unique characteristics are needed in a scrying speculum if it is to be effective. The important features of a speculum are as follows.

Clarity—The medium of the speculum has an appearance of clarity that you can see through. This may be light or dark, but it gives the impression of transparency. When the scryer gazes at it, there is a sense of passing through its surface and descending into it.

Depth—The speculum gives the impression of looking down a hole or progressing down a corridor or tunnel. There is a three-dimensional feel to the speculum when the seer is scrying into it.

Shape—The shape of the speculum is usually round or roundish. Square speculums are used but are not as common. The roundness facilitates the sense of going deeper into the speculum and is probably better for most beginners.

Reflection—The surface of the speculum must be at least partially reflective of the environment. The reflections give the mind something to work with. The eyes and mind do not work in a vacuum, but instead cause subtle, or not so subtle, changes in reflections present in the scrying medium.

Materials—The materials used vary, but speculums are generally made of glass, silver, crystal, or liquids such as water or quicksilver. In general, they are shiny, reflective, or transparent. Modern technology such as old television screens, computer screens, or phone screens can also be used. They are associated by the modern scryer with sources of information. Some beginners may have an easier time working with that established association.

Occult Associations—In addition to these physical qualities, speculums can have esoteric characteristics that are traditionally believed to increase their effectiveness for scrying. These can include such things as esoterically significant materials, naturally formed objects, occult links, symbolic shapes, and so on. I generally steer away from esoteric qualities. Relying on occult links may help some practitioners, but the boost is subtle and such associations are not universally agreed upon. When I do sessions with various different objects, I do not find any change in effectiveness related to occult associations. Scrying is not mystical; it is not really even all that esoteric. It is related to natural physiology and mental training.

Crystal Balls

Crystal and glass balls are popular choices for speculums. I recommend clear glass or crystal, but a slight tint of color is fine. A way to check how you react to color is to look at a color photo of the glass or crystal ball. If you get a sense of going deeper within it, then it will probably work for you. When you are looking for a crystal ball, scrying using photographs of crystal balls will help you to find the right one.

The cost of a crystal ball will vary depending on how big it is, its quality, what it's made of, and how it was manufactured. I have used balls of obsidian, leaded glass, processed quartz, and natural quartz. Obsidian is an opaque, naturally formed volcanic glass. Quartz is a transparent rock crystal that may be as clear as water or tinted with various colors such as milky white or rose. All but the obsidian balls work well for me. I have not used acrylic globes, since they are about the same price as glass, and acrylic is a soft material that becomes cloudy when its surface gets scratched up from friction in a bag or purse. I would suggest using a harder material that can be carried without being damaged and can be easily polished.

These crystal balls vary in size from marbles around an inch in diameter to large globes of as much as eight or ten inches. In shape they range from perfect spheres to egg-shaped ovals, and some may be faceted like large jewels. I do not recommend faceted crystal balls, nor do I recommend those that have a flat spot to keep them from rolling off the table. The larger sizes tend to be easier to use; however, large crystal or glass globes are not convenient to carry. A diameter of around two inches (about fifty millimeters) is a convenient size to carry and works well enough.

Natural quartz is probably the most popular material with New Age crowds, but other traditions use other materials. I do not personally find any difference in performance between quartz and glass when scrying. I have done experiments with various different materials and have found no measurable difference in accuracy from one session to another when scrying black-and-white, hit-or-miss types of targets. One of the best speculums I have used is the glass stopper of a lead crystal bottle. It is round in size and shape, much like a clear marble. I see more in that little round stopper than I do in many of my more expensive crystals. Lead is not an element usually associated with scrying, but sometimes things will work well that you would not think of as being good scrying tools.

Mirrors

The second most popular choice for a speculum is a mirror. Black mirrors, which have a black backing rather than a silvery backing, are seen quite a bit online and in stores; however, I do not favor black mirrors of glass or obsidian (volcanic glass) as a scrying material, because these materials cannot be used in a bright room. The room has to be dimly and evenly lit or you get a distracting glare. You need to be able to write when you are scrying most of the time, and complete darkness or candlelight is not conducive to good record keeping.

I recommend clear glass and a silver backing for your mirror. I was trained to scry on a silvered mirror angled to reflect only the ceiling. It is the size and shape of a cosmetic mirror, about three inches in diameter. It is flat, stores easily, and works for public situations where I wish to be discreet. It does not have any special features. I purchased a pack of these mirrors at a craft store. They can be ordered online for a few dollars. I suggest that you use a round shape. Square mirrors tend to have sharp corners that catch on things, which is a minor drawback. The scrying mirror can be supported with cardboard or a piece of wood—I use modeling clay to angle it.

Mirrors of various types of polished metal such as gold, copper, bronze, and tin have been used historically for scrying, but silver has been the most popular. I have tried scrying with gold leaf but did not have much success with it. Silver gives me better results. The advantage of a silvered mirror is that it is superior to any other kind of speculum in a bright room. I find glare to be distracting, and with the proper angling of the silvered mirror, glare can be completely eliminated even in sunlight.

Bowls

Another traditional scrying tool is a bowl, usually made of metal, but it can also be made of glass or crystal. This type of speculum includes such vessels as drinking glasses, wine glasses, and so on. The bowl is filled with water or some other liquid. Scrying is done with the clear bowl at eye level, with the metal bowl below your desk top or writing level. You gaze through the side of the clear bowl and down into the top of the metal bowl. The metal bowl should be about an arm's length away from your face.

The great French seer Nostradamus used a bronze bowl filled with water to scry his prophecies. Silver is traditional for a scrying bowl, but I find the glare to be too bright and annoying. A clear or darker bottom to the bowl works better for me. I use an old glass fishbowl that I picked up at a second-hand store. It's the kind you see at carnivals that you throw ping-pong balls into in order to win a fish. This fish bowl works well even in rooms that are brightly lit. I can use it filled with water or with nothing in it.

A cup of black coffee or tea actually works pretty well, as long as it is not too strong, although it does create a glare. Green tea is the best choice here. It has subtle color and it creates the illusion of depth without the glare that black tea and coffee create.

Lighting Considerations

When doing scrying in a bright room, the speculum should be partially covered to reduce glare. I use a small cloth about the size of a washcloth for this purpose. The material should be smooth, tightly woven, and without texture. When scrying into a clear bowl, the cloth can be placed behind the bowl to block some of the light, or partially stretched over the bowl, if care is taken not to allow it to touch the surface of the water. I use the cloths that my crystal balls are stored in as a partial cover when working with crystal balls. If you are in stealth mode, try using a cup of green tea as your speculum, and shade it with your hand or a coffee cup lid. You gaze into the area of the tea that is exposed and look toward the darker areas that are shaded by the cover.

Lighting is an important factor when working with speculums. Traditionally, rooms were lit with firelight and candles or oil lamps. In modern times, electric lights prevail. Electric lighting is harder to work with than candlelight or lamplight. Ideally there should be some flickering variation in the light. The flickering helps create motion in the vision. However, most of the time this may not be available.

You can learn to compensate for lighting that is less than ideal. One way is to use a silver cosmetic mirror. It seems to work best in a bright room with electrical lighting. The mirror can be used for stealth scrying, but green tea for a speculum is more subtle and less likely to draw comment. Both forms work well with electric lighting.

Gazing at the Speculum

The technique you use with a traditional speculum is to stare at it steadily until you see flashes, speckles, and streaks in your field of vision while looking at it. You want to mentally explore the depths of the device, and should think of it as a tunnel leading to the location you want to examine. The key is to be steady. Edward Kelley, an English scryer of the sixteenth century with whom I established communication, taught me to avoid blinking while doing this. Your eyes become tired quickly when you stare steadily, which is what you want in order to help induce visions. The idea is to keep your gaze fixed without moving your eyes. This forced stare was probably the original method for teaching scrying.

I have found that ever since the time I was working with Kelley, I do not have to force-stare to get an image. Steadiness of the eyes and body, as well as focusing on going deep into the speculum, are all that is needed to induce the external vision. Once you get the hang of this steadiness, you begin to see things like streaks, graying out, sparkles, and other visual aberrations. These appearances are not much different from those that arise during rice-matrix scrying.

What to Expect during a Speculum Scrying Session

The images you see in the speculum are usually very subtle. Scrying is mostly an optical effect that you interpret as vision. It is due to false images affecting the optic nerves in your eyes after you stare at something for a while—a natural biological response to the lack of stimuli that appears as a zoning out or blanking out of what you are gazing at. This response is involuntary, but it can be induced and controlled somewhat by a steady, unmoving gaze and a soft, unfocused vision. The scrying data is in the lines, shapes, colors, and activity present in those impressionistic visions. The challenge for this kind of scrying is to realize what the data looks like when you see it.

A minority of scryers will experience something like a dream or movie. However, most practitioners have to work with a more subtle sort of image. The image has the appearance of analog TV static with a faint TV picture, so that you have to almost use your imagination to see what is in there. There may be occasional images that flash. Most of the time it looks like shadows moving about the speculum. Some people will see in color, some will not. It is the description and study of these moving shadows that you need to work with when you do speculum scrying.

The movie-like experience does not seem to be more accurate than the subtle impressionistic visions. It is essential to accept the subtle moving shadows as being important. If you do this, you will open the door, so to speak, and be able to use this subtle effect to perceive data from the target and the points of primary information.

The best approach is to accept what you receive as a perception and work with that, rather than trying to make your body do something it is not designed to do. Everyone can scry, but the appearance in the speculum is unique to each individual. If you have vivid visuals, the challenge then becomes control and preventing visual labeling. Identifiable objects and events seen in this way are symbolic and dreamlike. They will probably relate to the aspects of primary information, but it may take some time and effort to figure out how that inner symbology works. This is the challenge for the scryer who experiences visual intensity.

The challenges the scryer faces are different with the two different types of vision. The scryer who experiences a subtle vision will have less difficulty with accuracy but may have trouble getting a handle on the data as it appears to them. The scryer with a vivid visual experience will have more difficulty with labels and accuracy but will not have any trouble perceiving the data. In this case it is more an issue with control.

The Speculum Scrying Session

You now have all the background you need and are ready for a traditional scrying session with a speculum. Clear a small area, even if it is just you sitting comfortably in a chair. Mentally set aside any distractions and focus on the session. Have something to write with. The traditional speculum scrying session will be very similar in format to that of casting and Tarot scrying.

Step One: The Grab Bag

Focus on opening to your subject of inquiry. You should be working with a hidden question from the grab bag. This rule applies for scrying concrete, physically based inquiries.

Step Two: Determine the Points of Primary Information

The speculum scrying session will begin with determining the points of primary information, just like with internal scrying. Follow the procedure described in chapter 2. Remember, primary information points can be *object*, *liquid*, *presence*, or *activity/energy*. You will pick three to start the session. Draw the box on your sheet of paper and place three points inside it. Pick which primary information point you want to explore first. Work with one point at a time. This will take you through a fifteen-minute session.

Step Three: Scrying the Primary Information Points

You have your speculum in front of you, angled or draped to avoid glare. You gaze into it. Study and look beyond the surface of the speculum into its depths. Feel yourself extending into those depths. Keep your body relaxed and still, and your gaze steady and unwavering. Initially I had to consciously prevent my eyes from blinking to get the steadiness I needed. After a while, I realized that you can achieve the same result as long as you mentally and physically keep very still and open. That is probably the hardest part of doing speculum scrying. It requires a steadiness to be maintained for at least a couple of minutes. Eventually you will start to see shadows.

Usually the shadows appear as though they are behind a veil of light. Let that subtle image grab your eyes. The suggestions of shapes and shadows you see in the speculum will eventually match the point of primary information that you are focusing on. This can happen very quickly. I did a couple of sessions on video just to see how long it takes—it can be somewhat difficult to gauge time accurately when you are scrying. It took only a minute or so for the shapes to appear.

If you read the Enochian diaries of Dr. John Dee, you will note that at times the visions scryed by Edward Kelley took thirty or more minutes to appear. I believe there were even sessions during which they waited a couple of hours before Kelley saw anything. This was probably due to the mental state of Kelley at the time. He was a heavy drinker and was doing alchemical experiments that exposed him to neurotoxic chemicals. He had symptoms of toxicity, including severe headaches. It is possible he was also medicating himself with various remedies for these problems. The chemical exposure appeared to be detrimental to his intuitive work. To scry well, the mind needs to be clear and you need to be able to describe and remember what you see.

Step Four: Recording the Session

This is a bit tricky. The scryer can do one of two things. If you are in a situation where you can record your session on video or at least record the audio, then you can describe verbally what you are seeing in the speculum. This is the easiest way to do a scrying session. It also allows you to extend the session if you want to do more detailed work. I use a digital voice recorder that I have previously used for radio channeling. The newer phones have voice-recording capabilities. You can use them as well. Once the session is finished, you can then transcribe the results if you wish. Sketching, as always, is the best way to record what you see.

The second method for recording a session is to remember what you saw in the speculum and then write it down or sketch it immediately after the session is finished. You can also sketch as you go, but you must not look at your paper while you are doing it—your gaze must remain on the speculum. It is best to jot a couple of things down quickly as you scry and then complete your notes after you finish with that primary information point.

I have tried working with both sketches and jotted notes and by verbally describing visual perceptions into a voice recorder. The recorder method captures more detail than sketching during the session. If you have to sketch your session and are in a place where you cannot make a voice recording easily, be sure the paper is taped securely to the table so that it does not move around.

Break Down Mental Labels

If you are scrying and see something in the speculum that can be identified— for example, if you see an outline that reminds you of a tree or a house—this is a mental label. Identifiable objects that appear in scrying visions are *usually* symbolic. These labels should be broken down into descriptive terms in order to understand the important content that the images contain.

I suggest that you work through each identifiable perception that comes up in the session. The image identified as a mental label is broken down into descriptive terms. For example, suppose I see a women's fan in the scrying mirror. The point I am exploring is an object. I ask, "How is this aspect of the primary information (*object*) related to this fan?" I then write down the answer to that question according to my internal intuition. I might write, "It is white, curve-shaped, small, hand-held, thin, pretty, and lightweight."

Usually, when you go back to study that particular point of primary information in the feedback, you will find that the description of the "fan" that you saw in the speculum fits some aspect of the target. The identifiable image is seldom literally present at the target site. Even if you occasionally have accurate and literal visions of the inquiry site, you should still make it a habit to break down the identifiable imagery into descriptive terms. It will cause you to become more accurate in the long run, and the level of detail in your sessions will improve.

Breaking down the mental labels will help you understand the symbolism of your deeper mind. I do not use symbol dictionaries for this purpose. I always break down my labels as I just explained. It is possible over time to build up a personal symbol dictionary of sorts between your deeper mind and your conscious awareness. You will start to notice some consistencies in the relationship between the deeper-mind symbols and the primary information aspects. This may be true particularly for those who tend to see dreamlike imagery in the speculum. You can make notes of the symbols and their relationships to tangible targets, and over time these notes will make for an effective and accurate symbol dictionary.

However, even if this is a possibility for you, the labels should still be broken apart into descriptive terms to gain greater detail and maintain accuracy. Any time you play with labels without breaking them down, regardless of your level of experience, you will be at risk of falling into a trap that results in an inaccurate session. The personal dictionary of symbols you compile should not be employed until you do the session analysis. Never analyze while scrying. Only describe the vision.

General Advice for Speculum Scrying

Scry a point of primary information until you feel you have enough information, then break contact before starting another point. The break doesn't have to be long, just a few seconds to reset before scrying another aspect. Training your eyes to form visions quickly is done by practice. If the images do not appear in the mirror, they will sometimes come to the scryer's imagination (internal scrying). This information should be described in words and sketched.

Eventually your deeper mind will figure out how to project the information into the speculum. With most classes, I find that this happens after a session or two. It is not so much that the image does not appear, but that you do not recognize that you are looking at the image. You see a shadow and think, "Oh, that is just a shadow," instead of allowing the variation in lighting to form shapes and motion. Beginners tend to look for a movie. If you start treating the shadows as significant, they will form the shapes and activity of the primary information aspects you are focusing on.

The initial response of beginners, when the blurring occurs and the shadows start moving, is to wiggle the body and blink. If you can avoid this while remaining relaxed, then the deeper images will start to come through. The most accurate images are usually subtle and are merely suggestive of an image, rather than something that looks perfectly clear. You may also find that you see the hints of images in the mirror but at the same time receive perceptions through internal scrying. Try to write down both types of perceptions. Do not worry about separating them—they come from the same source. Just let the perceptions arise as they will and how they will. If you focus on speculum scrying, you will be able to find the information in the speculum with a little practice. Focus on the perceptions rather than how they are being perceived.

If you use the speculum for a focus but find that your perception is all internal, this is also fine. There are a few people who have trouble using an external speculum. If you find that you are frustrated with it, just go to internal scrying or casting. There is nothing wrong with this. I have yet to meet anyone who cannot do internal scrying. In fact, you don't even need to believe in it to do it. You just have to follow the directions.

There is little preparation that needs to be done outside of the usual session setup procedure. You do not have to spend hours meditating. Meditation is useful for learning to sit still and focus, but aside from that it doesn't really contribute much to scrying skills. Meditate to learn about yourself, but to learn scrying you need to practice scrying. Nothing else will substitute for it. Some practitioners like to meditate and others do not. I fall somewhere in between. I have times when I feel it is beneficial and other times when it seems to be a waste of time and energy. I try to go with the flow and allow my intuition to guide me. I do not fight with it. My progress in scrying does not appear to relate at all to my meditation practice or lack thereof.

Eyelid Scrying

I want to go over how to do traditional scrying in a situation where you do not have privacy or a place to set up a speculum. Scrying against closed eyelids is the ultimate in stealth scrying. In closed-eyelid scrying, you allow images to form on the inner surface of your eyelids when your eyes are closed. It is not the same as imagination. The images are no different from those you will see in a speculum. It is one of the most useful methods to learn because it can be employed in field work. I rely on this method to see nature spirits while I am walking in the woods. When physical vision is cut off by closing the eyes, the spirit vision is allowed to reach conscious awareness. I learned to do this kind of scrying before I was able to use a speculum successfully.

The challenge of eyelid scrying is to learn to form the images quickly. You can write down impressions while you are doing this, but your paper has to be secured and you must write without looking at it. The other option is to remember what you saw and write it down after you are done. Even in covert sessions, I recommend that you write down the data as soon as you finish the session. A digital voice recorder can be used for the purpose of taking notes, but it is not very stealthy. It's best to train yourself to remember what you scryed. An advantage of eyelid scrying, aside from the stealth aspect, which allows you to scry in a situation where it would normally be impossible to use traditional scrying methods, is that it works well in brightly lit rooms.

Eyelid scrying is closer to speculum scrying than to internal scrying. It uses impressions seen when you close your eyes. With internal scrying, you are using your imagination—it is like a daydream. With eyelid scrying, you actually see some faint impressions or some shadowy images at times. Eyelid scrying is easier on your eyes than traditional scrying is. This is particularly true if you have a problem with dry eyes or are prone to eye irritation. It is easier to maintain a steady gaze and stillness of the body when you are comfortable. Your eyes do not dry out when you scry with them closed. Some people who have trouble working with a physical speculum have more success with eyelid scrying.

My earliest scrying impressions, such as those of a homunculus that called itself "People" and those of the Elizabethan scryer Edward Kelley, were seen by scrying with closed eyelids. Some of my best work has been done with this technique. You can work longer and harder with eyelid scrying than with conventional speculum scrying. You may want to switch to this method if you are experiencing fatigue, dryness, or achiness in your eyes when using a speculum in order to extend a traditional session.

The Eyelid Scrying Session

The procedure for eyelid scrying is the same as when scrying with a traditional speculum. The first step is to use the grab bag system to find your inquiry. Four distinct inquiries or four distinct questions on one inquiry should be in the bag. Pull out your slip of paper and set it aside in a safe place.

The next step is determining your points of primary information. Make your square, put your pen or pencil on three different points, and determine what primary information is at each point.

Once you have three primary information aspects, move on to scry these points. The same rules apply—you are looking mainly for shape, texture, activity, and color. Write down other perceptions you experience, even though they may not be visual. Set aside anything that is a label or an identifiable image. You can break those down at the end of the session.

It is best to try to write without looking at your paper. Try not to interrupt your gaze until you finish with the aspect you are working on. The outward appearance of you doing a session is basically someone who is meditating or thinking about something. Unless you speak, you can do this entirely without being noticed.

When you have an opportunity, and before you do your feedback, recopy your notes. Writing without looking at your paper is usually messy and not very legible. If you rewrite your notes in an orderly manner after the session is complete, you will not lose information.

Esoteric Inquiries

The setup for esoteric inquiries is a little different. An esoteric inquiry is a study of your inner mental, emotional, and spiritual environment. It is also a scrying study of a subject that is spiritual in nature, with little or no material representation. An esoteric inquiry will focus on a sigil or other symbolism that cannot be obscured. For your first few scrying sessions, I recommend that you avoid esoteric inquiries and work instead with concrete subjects of inquiry. Scrying the Kabbalistic Tree of Life is an example of an esoteric inquiry. Subjects such as Enochian angels, or grimoires such as the *Heptameron* of Peter de Abano, are esoteric in nature.

In situations where you have to have a specific setup for a scrying session that involves spirit communication, you need some verification that you are channeling and working accurately or that the spirit is being straight with you. In a grimoire-type séance, the inquiry of the spirit should contain a hidden target. For example, say you want to conjure Archangel Michael using the essay "The Art of Drawing Spirits into Crystals" that appears in Francis Barrett's book *The Magus* as your grimoire. You have to set up the session on a certain day and with specific equipment parameters that are in sync with Michael's energies. For this reason, you cannot hide the archangel as a target. However, what you can do is have a few questions in the grab bag and have the angel answer the questions while they are hidden from you so that you are relying entirely on the communication for information.

Instead of you scrying the questions directly, the angel is scrying them and telling you the data. The spirit should give you the data in the same format that you use for scrying—that is, by using descriptions and avoiding labels. Angels and other spirits see the world in a different way than someone who lives here physically does. Relying on the format where you avoid labels and instead use descriptions, as you were instructed to do for your scrying sessions, will give you much more accurate information from the spirit. When you are doing spirit communication, you will have to learn to accept a margin of error similar to what you experience when doing direct scrying.

You can improve the accuracy of your spirit communication in two ways: first by using hidden inquiries, and second by having the spirit give descriptions of the events, people, and locations you are asking about. Dowsing can be done with the spirit to help facilitate the acquisition of information that is appropriate to that technique. Spirits can also help you with scrying. Regardless of how you work with the spirit, the principles should be the same as when you are doing your own scrying. Doing a séance and working with a spirit is an interesting experience. However, a spirit cannot do anything more than you can do on your own with the proper technique and development. As with all other types of scrying, feedback is critical to improvement and continued accuracy in your work.

Recap of the General Procedure for Speculum Scrying
Scrying sessions can be done anywhere and under almost any conditions. You develop your understanding of how to scry only with practice. That is

how you improve your scrying skills. In closing this chapter, let's go over the general procedure one more time to make sure you understand all the steps.

1. Have your subjects ready. Draw one from the grab bag. No peeking!
2. If you are using physical tools, get them out. Have something with which to record the session.
3. Determine the points of primary information. Pick the aspects you think are most important to start with.
4. Study the crystal or mirror with a relaxed body and a steady gaze. Record the visual aberrations you see, as well as whatever impressions come to your mind. Break contact, pick another primary information point, and then do it again until all three primary information aspects are worked through.
5. Do your feedback session.

CHAPTER TEN

CASE STUDIES
IN SPECULUM SCRYING

In this chapter I will present two actual case studies from my own work records to illustrate how the various tools of scrying are to be applied in a practical way during scrying sessions. The illustrations have been redrawn to render them more legible so that their content can be understood. In actual scrying sessions, sketches are made rapidly without looking at the paper, and tend to be difficult for anyone other than the scryer to interpret.

Case Study One: Sable Island

The selection of the inquiry was from four unique targets. I selected the paper containing the information and set it aside without looking at which question I would be working with. For the sake of the case study, the inquiry is presented first, but bear in mind that it was not known at the time of the scrying session.

Subject of Inquiry

On Sable Island, a national wildlife preserve off the coast of Nova Scotia, there is a small research facility consisting of a couple of buildings and a weather station. This island is particularly vulnerable to rising sea levels, as it is basically a sandbar with sparse vegetation, migratory birds, and gray seals. The most famous animal life on the island is a herd of feral horses, which are the descendants of horses left on the island by ships two hundred years ago. Somehow these horses managed to survive and breed, and over the generations have become very hardy, but if the sea level rises as much as has been predicted, this island will become uninhabitable for all large animals, human and horse alike, and may end up being completely under water.

The target was the weather research facility on Cape Sable Island two hundred years into the future from the time of writing. This is what would be classed as a partially esoteric project. Some of the information gathered will be verifiable and some will not. This is a suitable scrying project for an intermediate to advanced scryer.

Tasking Statement

"Scry Sable Island in the year 2219 to determine the state of the island and whether it will be partially or wholly under water at that time."

The Scrying Session

The session took about ten minutes. The speculum used was an ordinary drinking glass from the kitchen filled with water. It was not made of any special materials, and had never been set apart for ritual or divination use. The water was ordinary tap water from the well.

The Lighthouse Ritual (described in chapter 13) can be used on this subject since there are some aspects of this inquiry that are physically at the location in the present time and are likely to still be there two hundred years from now in some form or another. I will use these features to help form and reinforce the neural pathways to accurate scrying.

The points of primary information are *object*, *liquid*, and *presence*. I hear a hissing that sounds train-like (figure 10.1). In light of the inquiry, it is likely to be the sound of wind and sea. This is possibly evidence of a high wind and could indicate a hurricane.

First, in the speculum, I see a building with someone standing in front of it. The figure appears much like the Hermit of the Rider-Waite Tarot deck. This is a visual label. I feel that this presence is actually at the location. The emotional state is alone or lonely. There is a notable absence of artificial lighting, mechanical noises, or other indications of electricity, which could mean that the generator is not being used or is not available. There is a structural object of some kind behind the presence. It has a steeply pitched top, much like a church in appearance. I feel that the number of presences at this location is lower than expected. The number of people on the island is probably between four to eight at the present time. The house is large enough for about eight people. Horses and seals would also come across as a presence in the process of examining the aspect of *presence*, but I do not pick up anything that appears to be the presence of large animals at the location on the future date.

Figure 10.1: Sable Island

Next I see a layered structure and feel a tremendous downward pressure on it. This I interpret as water. Sable Island is known for its multiple shipwrecks. It is not clear to me if this is a shipwreck or one of the structures that was at one time present on the land. I see a male figure with a moustache. He has dark hair. Next I see some structures that appear to be ruins or in ruin. The *presence* breaks down to "dark on top, rough, lonely, bipedal, and living in a primitive situation."

I did not pick up any presences that appeared to be or sounded like horses. I also only picked up three humanlike presences. I could see that one was male. He appeared in the speculum with dark hair and a large moustache and mutton chops. He had a broad face with mostly Celtic features. There was a clear vision of the face of this presence in the speculum. As I scry, I feel that it is symbolic of a sailor and a person who lives in the rough as a way of life. It does not carry the presence of someone who would be a scientist or someone who works with weather experiments. It is more like someone who lives on a boat year-round, such as a fisherman.

I do not know the gender of the others present, or if they were living there at the targeted time of the scrying. Only the male with the mutton chops appeared present at the time in context with the building. The object in his hand for lighting seemed to indicate a lack of power at the location and primitive conditions. The station is presently powered by diesel generators. Attempts to install other types of power at the station have failed due to the isolation and harshness of the climate. The weather station requires electric power, so this is possibly symbolic of the deterioration of the research facility.

It does not appear to be winter. The research teams inhabiting Sable Island are evacuated if there are dangerous storms in the area. The horses and other wildlife are, however, always there—the herd is considered feral and is not moved from the island. The main residential house of the research station is consistent with the shape of the structure I saw.

In this session I would interpret the information gathered to show a normal course of events. The station did not appear to be submerged. Some of the buildings have endured for two hundred years, and some have fallen apart. This would be expected in this time frame without catastrophic effects of sea-level rise. I think a slow deterioration of the research facility will occur over the next couple of hundred years. It could be due to climate, or it could just be due to lack of funds to continue the program.

The wild horses may or may not still be there. I cannot say for sure that they are gone. The focus of the session was on the research facility. The animals may simply have been in a different location at that time. They may have died off from other causes if they are not present. Inbreeding issues and the weather issues Sable Island is prone to will eventually make the equestrian herd nonviable.

Dowsing Session

An either-or dowsing question was composed to further clarify the result of the scrying session: "Will the differences seen in the Sable Island research station be due to (A) water-level rising and natural causes (even number) or (B) natural causes without water-level change (odd number)?"

My feelings before the dowsing: I think it's a hard call. I do think the sea levels may be expected to rise, but I'm not sure how much that is actually going to affect the landscape. My feeling is uncertain and neutral. The scrying session emphasized natural causes and a slow deterioration, which could be due to the passage of time and a lack of funding.

A square is drawn on paper, and a cross drawn through it to divide it into four equal smaller squares. A series of dots are made rapid-fire with the pen and distributed without counting them or thinking about them over the entire surface of the larger square, by moving the pen around the intersection of the cross.

The first quadrant contains fourteen dots, an even number, which indicates that A is the response. The second number is twelve; this also points to A. The third quadrant contains nine dots, which indicates B. The fourth quadrant has eight dots, which selects A as its response. The overall response is A. It appears that there is going to be a change in sea level along with the other natural causes that will bring about deterioration of living conditions on Sable Island.

This clarification by dowsing helps illuminate the prediction and is consistent with what would be expected. The results are not out of line with current science. I do think there may be harsher conditions present on Sable Island in the next couple of hundred years. The horse herd could die out. Due to genetic issues, this die-out would not be unexpected, even if the island is still intact two centuries from now. The weather station there will likely deteriorate and could become irreparable due to harsh weather and sea level fluctuations. The main house will be maintained, perhaps as a sea rescue base. The rest of the facility appears to be in ruins. This deterioration could be gradual, or it could be sudden and violent, the result of a hurricane hit. I'm inclined to go with a gradual deterioration and failure to keep up with repairs.

Case Study Two: The Great Sphinx

In this case study, I initiated the session in the same way I did for the case study on the future of Sable Island. The subject was randomly selected using the grab bag technique. The question remained hidden until after the session. I will present the inquiry subject first, even though it was not known to me during the scrying session.

Subject of Inquiry

The Great Sphinx in Egypt is alleged to have underground chambers that, according to famed seer Edgar Cayce, hide ancient secrets of human history. Recent excavations have revealed that there is something under the Sphinx. I wanted to uncover the secrets of that room, if it exists.

Tasking Statement

"Look inside and underneath the Great Sphinx. Describe documents and other artifacts of interest that rest in rooms or tunnels at that location. If any have been removed, describe what was formerly present under there."

Session Summary

This was a very interesting target to me, since I have read some of the accounts of the Sphinx and conspiracy theories that the Ministry of Antiquities in Egypt is hiding artifacts and information about this ancient monument. The session was highly visual, more so than the last session on Sable Island. I used an ordinary drinking glass and common well water for this session. The glass used was a small, clear juice glass from the kitchen. It was not made of any special materials, nor was it selected for any specific reason.

Scrying Session

I found primary information points of *object*, *liquid*, and *presence*. As illustrated in figure 10.2, I saw a boxy structure with layered brick-like construction around it. It was next to a ribbon of water. In fact, there was a lot of water here considering that this is supposed to be a desert. I felt a very strong water-land interface here. It was not dry. I had another target in the grab bag of the Amazon Basin, and as I was doing the session I found that I was guessing that it was the Amazonian target. This is not uncommon when you have hidden targets. This is why it is important to focus on the aspects of primary information and not go into a story line about the guess that is wandering in your head. If I had not stayed with the session structure and remained focused on the points of primary information, the session would not have been accurate. But because I did stay with the structure, the session provided some very interesting data.

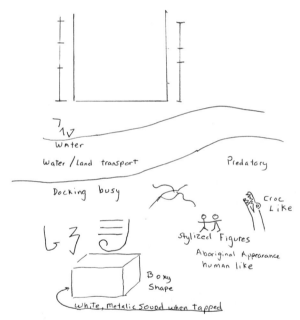

Figure 10.2: The Great Sphinx, First Sketch

I perceived a stylized painting of someone with dark skin and dark eyes. I saw a small metallic object that was boxy and painted white. This object, shown in the first sketch, was below and on the other side of the water interface. In terms of the modern geology of Egypt and the Nile, this does not make any sense. I had impressions of a couple of stylized images: one of a crocodile and the other of two humans linked together.

In figure 10.3, there is a mushroom-shaped object and the words "poisoned toadstool" at the side. I think this is symbolic of something that was toxic, or made toxic, that is related to the subject of inquiry. I also saw something that looked like a measurement or measuring device, and understood the words "Make it taller" and "Get out." I also heard a tapping sound similar to a mason's hammer.

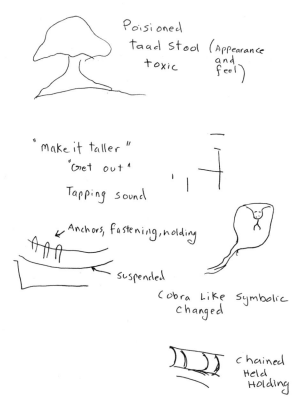

Figure 10.3: The Great Sphinx, Second Sketch

Next to this, I have an object that didn't make much sense to me. It was in some ways similar to a suspension bridge. It was not really rigid and appeared to be made of rope. It had anchors in several places and was related to water somehow. I'm not sure what the relationship was of this object to water. There was also a cobra-like symbol associated with this. It was an area where there were active presences and active construction or work-like activity. The cobra is depicted on the pharaoh's crown, but I don't know if that was the case at this time in the past. I'm not sure what the cobra symbolized. I sense that this place has really changed since the Sphinx was built.

Interpretation

I think that this monument may be a tomb. It appears that the water levels and course have changed through the years. There are paintings in chambers below at the very least. The box is about the right size and shape for a coffin, though it is not the usual design. There may be something inside this box that is of interest or is related to the topic. The cobra and crocodile are certainly symbols consistent with ancient Egypt. In this case, the cobra and crocodile were not identified as such, but are used as descriptive terms related to the object aspect of primary information. The concept of stylized figures includes the crocodile in figure 10.2. These are not broken down, because they are descriptive of appearance rather than an object that I believed was at the site. I wrote "croc-like," meaning it looks similar to a crocodile, and "cobra-like," meaning it looks like a cobra in shape. I am using the nouns as adjectives in this situation. It is okay to do this, though for a beginner I would suggest breaking these down even though they are descriptions and not actual objects perceived at the location. The crocodile-like and cobra-like appearances are probably symbolic and are a good example of scrying symbolism as it appears in session.

I feel overall that I didn't get deep enough into the target to really get at the information I was looking for. The first sketch in figure 10.2 does indicate to me that there is something significant under the Sphinx, and it may have even gone past and under the Nile River, though I do not think the course of this river then was even remotely similar to what it is now. Either that or there was another river that fed into the Nile at that location, and the Sphinx marked the meeting place of the two rivers. There was water right next to it, and lots of dock-type activity going on. This could possibly be a miss. Scrying is not completely accurate, and in this case study, I am showing that there is possibly an error here or something that does not agree with history as it has been preserved for us.

However, if the alternative opinion is accurate that the Sphinx is much older than is currently believed by mainstream archaeology, then the scrying would be spot-on, and that perception would not be a miss. The theory that the Sphinx is older holds that there is flood damage to the Sphinx. If the Sphinx was built at the intersection of two rivers, this would certainly make sense. The stylized images and symbols are very much in line with ancient Egyptian artistry.

Overall, this session had some very interesting results and leaves us with more questions than answers. I find this to be the case when scrying mysterious artifacts. You may get one question answered, but the data will leave you with twenty more questions that you did not have before the session.

CHAPTER ELEVEN
ALPHANUMERIC
DOWSING AND SCRYING

Alphanumerics are letters and numbers. They are present in almost every facet of modern life. They are also one of the most challenging concepts to scry or dowse. Alphanumerics are basically labels for abstract concepts. They function and have the same effect as labels do in session. This makes them an interesting challenge.

Alphanumerics that involve money are particularly difficult, as money has a high emotional investment for most people. Targets that have high emotional value are usually the most difficult from which to get accurate results. I have a couple of scrying and dowsing techniques that work fairly well when divining numerical values and letters, which I will present in this chapter. I will be talking about gambling targets. I do not advocate gambling. I use the games as target practice and nothing more.

The gambling industry feeds on the emotional high of risk-taking behavior. Once an emotional attachment is present—the anticipation of a win or fear of a loss—the ability to do scrying and dowsing diminishes. These arts are best practiced with targets that are emotionally neutral. Adding emotions and attachments will deteriorate scrying skills much in the same way labels do. They can also deteriorate your financial situation, as the setup for all gambling institutions is designed to part you from what little cash you may have by manipulating your thoughts and emotions.

That being said, gambling games are number games, and these are excellent practice for doing alphanumeric work. Games will sharpen your skill as a scryer and dowser. Lottery games, racing and team predictions, and games like roulette all have aspects that provide fertile practice for a scrying student. You do not need to use money and put yourself at financial risk to do this practice.

I practiced alphanumeric scrying for a couple of years, and occasionally still play with it. I found that it really helped my development as a psychic and increased the precision in my work. I also learned a hard lesson regarding burnout, and what happens when you push yourself too hard with this kind of work.

This chapter is based on what I learned from that experience. I have listed some benign and fun targets at the end. Playing with numbers and letters is interesting and can be fun as long as you do not burn yourself out on it. You learn a great deal about what works and what does not work. Alphanumeric inquiries are straightforward. Feedback is very easy to do with this kind of subject. These sessions are short, often five minutes or less.

Direct vs. Indirect Dowsing and Scrying

There are two basic approaches to scrying and dowsing alphanumerics: the direct approach and the indirect approach. Direct methods of working with alphanumeric values involve the scryer or dowser scrying and dowsing the letter or number without using anything else to represent the number or letter. In dowsing you are asking a yes-no question regarding the letter or number you are examining. If you are scrying, you are trying to find an impression of a letter or number in the speculum, in the casting material, or in your own mind.

Indirect dowsing and scrying is when you use something else that is easier to scry or dowse to represent the letter or number. Usually this is a photo-based target. It can be other things that are easier to work with than letters or numbers, such as shapes or colors.

Dowsing vs. Scrying

For most targets that are primarily number-based, such as sports team predictions, dowsing is the preferred method of working. Scrying can be done as well but requires a longer session. Pendulum dowsing is the easiest method to use. The second-best dowsing method is tapping with the squares.

Scrying numbers and letters usually works better if you use an indirect method. In my group practice the leader would set up a primary target, which was a stock prediction or a game involving two sports teams. We did not work with our financial/gaming targets directly in these experiments. The target was represented by two photos of tangible, grounded physical scenes, each of which indicated a particular outcome, such as "higher" or "lower" in the case of stocks, and "win" or "lose" in the case of a sports team. The photos were generated randomly and assigned by a computer program designed by the project manager. The photos were not in any way related to the target in appearance. Most of them were landscapes, portraits, and animals. I prefer using travel photos that are landscape in nature.

In these groups, photos were chosen to represent the targets, because they are easy for those trained in controlled remote viewing (CRV) and associative remote viewing (ARV) to work with. Most team members used CRV or ARV. CRV views the target directly, while ARV views the target through its association with something else. I was trained in both of these skills. However, because I was developing the scrying skills that I had learned from the spirit of Edward Kelley, I used scrying much of the time. We had a few dowsers in the groups as well.

The two photos representing a target were randomly generated by a computer, and were not known to us or the project manager prior to the session. We were told to "remote-view the outcome" of the upcoming event. We remote-viewed, scryed, or dowsed it according to personal preference. After we turned in our session, we would match the session data to one of the two photos that was revealed to us. We had to select the photo that our data most closely resembled. When we selected that photo, our prediction was made according to the parameters set up by the program. We did not know, nor did the project manager know, which photo represented which outcome for that prediction. This is called a double-blind target.

After the date of the event involved in the prediction had passed, we received our evaluation as to whether or not we had made a hit or a miss. The program also kept track of our statistics. This experience was with a highly sophisticated setup of the nature used in professional parapsychology experiments. There was no possibility of cheating or waffling. It was very black-and-white. The results were impressive and demonstrated clearly that groups are able to make accurate predictions.

Controlled remote viewing is a seven-step process first developed by Ingo Swann. It is more complex than scrying, and less interactive. CRV is rigidly structured, and that structure is followed almost slavishly. The data obtained by CRV is just as accurate as that gained through the scrying techniques I am teaching in this book; however, scrying is easier to learn and its structure is more flexible. Associative remote viewing can be done using scrying, even though the acronym ARV would not be correct in that case—the term associative scrying (AS) would be more accurate.

Picking Horse Race Winners

To discuss working with numbers, we will use a fictitious horse race. I did do actual sessions of this nature a few years ago, but I did not save the sessions to use as case studies. I will describe the procedure I used when working with this subject, which should demonstrate the technique adequately.

The horse races were harness-racing pacer stakes races that ran five to eight horses per race. Horses were numbered according to their post, or starting position, from the position nearest the inner rail of the racetrack (which is post position one) to the outside rail. The numbers were single digits going from one to eight. The average winning time at this trotting and pacing track, where the races are all one mile long, was right around two minutes.

Suppose I want to use dowsing to see if I can determine which horse will win a particular race. How can I set this up so I have a fighting chance at dowsing the correct answer? There are several ways to set up this target, but before we get to them, let's consider the value in hiding the target.

Hiding the Target of a Race

Making a hidden target out of this race is going to be difficult. On the other hand, unless my horse or my friend's horse is running in the race, I do not have any kind of attachment to any particular horse. Because I have no emotional attachment to the horses or the outcome, I can do direct dowsing of the race. If there were horses in there that represented an attachment of some sort, I would have to take care to hide my targets. If it is possible, hiding the target is helpful to accuracy. In some cases you can and in others you cannot. You have to work with the individual situations. Experimentation will reveal how much information you can handle without running into problems. In the following examples I explain how to hide the target for the prediction. It may, however, be too cumbersome to use at a live racetrack where you are sitting on a bench with no privacy.

First Technique: Direct Dowsing with a Number Line

The first option I have is to use a number line and directly dowse the winning horse by its post position number. I draw the number line on a blank page, off-center and at an angle, as I described in chapter 5. The numbers on the number line need to be the numbers of the post positions of the horses in the race. I cover the number line page with heavy blank paper that is the same size and shape as the page with the number line on it, and dowse the line using pins to mark the locations of the positive dowsing responses. I then transcribe the information to the number line. Feedback is done when the race is finished and the results are known. After you dowse a session, you need to make sure that you compare your results with the race outcome.

Do not get frustrated with misses. I find that I have a lot of near misses in which I was close to the winning horse but did not get it quite right. Observe your patterns and learn from them rather than belittling yourself for your lack of success. Emotional negativity will affect your ability in the same way as emotional excitement. You need to keep yourself neutral. There is a great deal you can learn from your misses that will help you be a more accurate scryer and dowser. It is more informative to study your misses than your hits. This is why the number games are so great for doing dowsing and scrying.

You get feedback, and the patterns you have are easier to observe because of the black-and-white nature of the targets.

Second Technique: Elimination Dowsing

The easiest way to do this technique is with index cards. Use a pencil to lightly mark the cards so that you can erase and reuse them. Take the stack of cards and put the numbers of the horses in the race on the cards. For eight horses, you should have eight cards, each with a number, one through eight. Shuffle the index cards so that you cannot see what is marked on them. Your tasking is to pick the post position number of the horse that wins this race. One card at time, dowse for a yes-no response.

You can use any indoor dowsing method we covered. If you are at the track, you will probably be sitting outdoors on a bench and will have to keep everything in your lap. You will probably want to be discreet. Usually when you dowse this way, you will get more than one positive response. Take the cards with a positive response and dowse again for the winner. For eight horses, it may take two to three eliminations to come up with the prediction.

Variation Using the Horses' Names

When you are working with horse-racing predictions, it is useful to experiment with dowsing more than one parameter. A second method is to do elimination dowsing by using the horses' names. In the racing schedule, each horse will be named. To do this elimination, put each name on an index card in light pencil so you can use the card again after erasing the name. The name has to be completely erased off the card before reusing it. Each racehorse has a unique name. Dowse the cards for the horse winning the race that you are working on. Eliminate the cards that have a negative response, and re-dowse the ones with a positive response until you come up with one card.

Once the race is run, compare your session with the race results. Look for patterns, such as predicting the horse to the left or right of the winning horse, or oppositional dowsing, where you pick the horse that comes in last instead of first. Identifying these patterns is important to help you gain more accuracy. Everyone has patterns like this, and it is important that you identify any patterns when you have a miss.

Variation Using Stable Colors

A third method that you should work with is the use of stable colors. Each stable usually has multiple horses. Hobby owners who may have only one or two horses usually send their racers to be trained with a larger stable, and they race under the colors of the training stable. The colors are sort of like the flags of countries. Stables are easily identified by their colors, and all horses racing under a particular stable's name will bear those colors. Usually it is the driver or jockey who wears clothing made with the colors of that stable. Most of the time two colors and a pattern are used.

For this method, we predict race results using stable colors. Since the average person will not know the patterns, the colors are more convenient. (I would use a color pattern chart made before I went to the race.) Use a color wheel for your chart. You can find these at art supply stores, or make one yourself by copying it from the internet. Disorient the chart by setting it off-center and at an angle. Cover it with a heavy opaque sheet of paper.

Tasking will be to identify one of the colors of the winning horse for that race. Use a pin to mark the spot where you have a positive response, and mark the information on another sheet of paper so you can reuse the color chart for other races. Once you have identified one color, you can identify another. Use the first color if the second color does not match anything in that race, and see how you do.

My best predictions have been made when using stable colors. Sometimes you will not see them in smaller races. If you do not have the stable colors available, then you cannot use this particular parameter for dowsing or scrying.

Dowsing the Winning Race Time

The winning time is also something you may want to try to dowse at a horse race, as an exercise to improve your skills. In this case, where we know that the winning time will be around two minutes, we will use that as our set point. The best method for doing this is a number line with the times on it. For trotter-pacer tracks, it's best to set 2:00 as the center point. Some tracks will be a little slower or faster than others. There is a possibility that the winning time will be over two minutes. If you are doing this with Thoroughbred racing, the time will be according to the length of the race. Eight furlongs is a mile. Trotters and pacers always race one mile. Thoroughbreds will race at various distances depending on the age of the horse and the type of race. Comparing your dowsing results to the race results will give you great feedback, and it will also help you identify your personal patterns in dowsing.

Scrying at the Horse Race

There are various options for setting up a scrying session at a horse race. I will go over a couple of them. The first is to try to scry the numbers. This is really challenging to do directly, but when you get a hit, it is also very gratifying. I would suggest scrying with a written tasking statement that contains the race information, such as the number of the race. I would use closed-eyelid scrying or internal scrying for this. Other methods could be used if you are working from home and watching a racing channel on a monitor or television screen.

What you are trying to scry are bits and pieces of the number. Hiding the target is not practical in this situation. You cannot have any emotional attachments to that race, either financially or to the horses, if you are to do this accurately. When you scry for a number, you will probably pick up fragments of the appearance of the number. In this situation you are working with labels. Numbers have the same effect as labels in session.

When you are ready to scry the race, start by drawing a square box on a sheet of paper, and set down three points of primary perception inside it. Scry the end of the race, since you may find yourself at the starting gate instead of the end if you do not specifically set your focus. Numbers show up as either energy or objects in the primary perception. Instead of looking at the other perceptions, pick out the *object* or the *energy/activity* perception. If it does not come up as either one of those, then you cannot scry that race. Take a short break and start with another race.

Describe the object or energy using the regular descriptive terms. Sketch any flashes you perceive that look like a line or curve. When you finish, study your sketches to see what number the lines and curves most resemble. That number is then your prediction. When you finish watching the race and the winner is declared, compare the number of the winner to the sketches and your interpretation. That is your feedback.

Environmentally Scrying the Starting Gate

Both Standardbred and Thoroughbred racing will use a starting gate to ensure a fair start to the race. Standardbred horses trot or pace in harness, with a driver behind in a cart. Thoroughbred horses are raced with a rider in the saddle on the horse's back at a gallop.

In a Standardbred race, the pacers and trotters move behind a vehicle that has two long arms. The horses have to follow the arms until they reach the starting line, at which point the arms retract and the race begins. The arms have on them the numbers of the horses, and the horse assigned to each number has to stay behind that number as they approach the start of the race.

In Thoroughbred racing, the horses are started from a standstill in a line of small starting stalls. Each horse is assigned a starting position and must go into that particular stall before the race begins. The stall door opens to the track and a bell goes off when the horses burst forth and begin their race.

You can use environmental scrying to scry the starting stalls to attempt to predict the winner of the race. You will be making the prediction quickly in this situation, since the race may be only a minute or two long. To do this, study each position on the gate and look for a shimmer above one number. This will be your prediction. This is easier to do with Thoroughbred racing than Standardbred, because the starting gates are out before the race starts. In a Standardbred race, the arms are not in position until they are taking the horses to the starting line. You will have only a few seconds to scry and make your prediction this way in a Standardbred race.

Scrying the Horses Warming Up

Prior to the race, the horses are warmed up and any issues with tack and other problems are ironed out. This happens just before the race. You can scry and attempt to make a prediction during this warm-up period. Use the environmental scrying technique, and look for a little shimmer above one of the horses. When you see the shimmer, that will be your prediction for the winner of that race. Make sure to do a good feedback session once you have the race results. Look for consistent patterns, especially with the misses.

Scrying Stable Colors

Closed-eye technique and internal scrying are the two methods of choice for scrying stable colors. The colors are the colors representing the training stable of each horse. This works very similarly to dowsing colors, except you will be attempting to scry the colors instead of dowsing them on a color wheel. The two techniques that can be used at the track, if you are physically there, are closed-eyelid scrying and internal scrying. Start your session by drawing a square and looking for three points of primary information. The focus will be on the end of the race. Be sure to specify this. If you have an *object* or *activity* primary perception, then scry that perception and look for one color at a time. Also note any shapes, as these are sometimes used as part of the identification of the stable.

Working in Groups

Group consensus is generally more accurate than individual results when working with monetary or numerical values. The larger the group the better, up to about a dozen people. More than that and the accuracy tends to level out and not increase with more participants. A neutral nonparticipating member of the group can compile and interpret the scrying data.

Indirect Scrying of a Binary Target

I want to mention indirect binary scrying because it is useful for scrying binary targets. A binary target is an event with two possible outcomes. This is applicable to team game predictions, most political election predictions, and market predictions. I will describe how to set up a binary target for scrying. The parameters are usually win-lose, above-below, greater than-less than, or more than-less than. If you want to do stock or bond market predictions, this is the best method to use.

To set up this kind of target, you need a group of A and a group of B targets. I have two sets of files with various travel photographs picked from the internet. The files are divided into two groups: the A pool and the B pool. Each photo has a number and a letter. They are divided into pairs so that number 1 has photos A and B, number 2 has A and B, and so on. Each number is assigned a pair of photos. This pool should have at least eight targets, four on the A side and four on the B side. A represents a positive result, such as "above," "win," or "greater than," and B stands for a negative result, such as "below," "lose," or "less than."

	File A (Win)	File B (Lose)
1.	Photo 1-A	Photo 1-B
2.	Photo 2-A	Photo 2-B
2.	Photo 3-A	Photo 3-B
4.	Photo 4-A	Photo 4-B

The subjects of the photos are not important, but the photos in each pair must be completely different from each other. I usually divide them according to the primary information aspects of *liquid* and *presence*. So if one photo has a great deal of water, then the one it is paired with might have a group of people and no water. The photos cannot be digitally altered; they have to be originals. Photoshopping images will put the focus on the person at the computer who did the artwork.

The primary target—say, a stock market prediction—is not hidden, but the photos that you will be scrying remain concealed. The photos represent outcomes. A is generally used for a "positive" or "increase" outcome, and B is used for a "decrease" or "negative" outcome.

To set up the session, pick the date you want to look at for your primary target, and the parameter you want to look at. This is your tasking statement, which you should write down. Let's say you want to examine local temperature. In that case, your set point would be the average temperature on that day of the year—for example, 50 degrees F.

The numbers one to four, written on identical folded slips of paper so that you cannot see what is marked on them, go into the grab bag. Draw a target out of the grab bag of indirect subjects, one of the numbers representing the A and B photos. If the response is above or on the average temperature, then you will scry and describe the A target of the number you have drawn. If the correct response is below the average temperature, then you will describe the B target. Because you are using the grab bag, you will not know when you do the scrying which target you are describing.

Only the numbers that label pairs of photos go into the grab bag. The photos should be kept in a computer file. I have a computer folder for the indirect scrying photos. Inside it are two subfolders labeled A and B. Inside those folders are the photos, which are numbered. Remember, only the number goes into the bag to allow you to reference the photo pair you are using for the scrying session. The number is not revealed until after the scrying session.

Example of Indirect Scrying

Let's say I want to predict the daily high temperature at my location during a period of one week. Historically, the known average high for this week is 50 degrees Fahrenheit. This becomes my set point. I have four numbers in the grab bag that are the scrying targets. Each target is linked to an A photo and a B photo. Photo A will be associated with the prediction that the daily high temperature for the week will be 50°F or greater. Photo B will be associated with the prediction that the daily high temperature will be below 50°F.

I will scry and describe photo A of my selected target if the daily high is going to be at or greater than 50°F, and photo B if the daily high will be below 50°F. It is the photos that represent higher than 50°F and below 50°F. They are the hidden representatives of the primary target, which is the daily temperature. It does not matter what the two representative photos are, as long as they are different from each other in appearance. Start the scrying session just like you do in a normal session. You will not know which representative photo you scryed until the end of the session, when you do your feedback.

After finishing the scrying session, compare the scrying data to the two representative photos, and match the session to one of those two photos. Look at each piece of data and determine if it is in photo A, photo B, or both. Then count up the number of perceptions that match A, the number that match B, and the number that match both. The representative photo with the most perceptions is the answer, so if you pick photo A and it is associated with the temperature above 50°F, then the prediction is that the temperature will be at or above 50°F on that day. For our purposes, let's say that photo A matched the scrying session better than photo B. The response is

50°F or above. I can either be satisfied with that answer or I can go to a new set point—say, 60°F—and repeat the procedure.

When doing binary targets with only two possible responses, this form of indirect or associative scrying is very accurate. It is usually more accurate than direct scrying, which is why I am teaching it here. Over time, you should compile a group of about one hundred photos if you want to do this kind of work more than occasionally. It is good scrying practice and it gives good results in making predictions. The type of predictions that I used this method for were mainly stock predictions and gaming predictions involving two-team games such as baseball, football, hockey, and soccer. I found that my accuracy of prediction using this method could be as high as 90 percent for short periods. The average was well over 60 percent. Most of the psychic groups I worked with used remote viewing. However, as I mentioned before, I was focused on reengineering and modernizing scrying techniques, so most of the time I used scrying instead of controlled remote viewing. The team members were allowed to use whatever techniques they wanted, and only the predictions and session summary were turned in.

Scrying Letters

In the Enochian diaries of Dr. John Dee, his professional scryer Edward Kelley spent hours at a time trying to scry series of individual letters. There were two main transmissions of this type that were recorded by Dr. Dee and later found their way into Meric Casaubon's *True & Faithful Relation*, a book that records the transcripts of their scrying sessions. The first was a table containing Enochian spirit names, and the second was a set of Enochian calls, or incantations, to be used with that table when conjuring the spirits of the table. The calls were said to be in the "Angelic" language.

Before he scryed this Great Table and the Enochian calls, Kelley worked on close to a hundred different tables. There may be tables missing from the diaries, so the number of tables could even be over a hundred. None of the tables had much in the way of usable practical function other than occult exploration until he scryed the Enochian Great Table. Then you see some practical functions associated with the table. It was an improvement over their previous work but still fell short of the goal of the experiments.

The goal of the scrying sessions and the focus of their work was to uncover the secrets of mineral alchemy—the transmutation of metals and gemstones. The sessions were interesting even before the Great Table and the calls were obtained, but the information obtained in the sessions was not consistently practical for the intended purpose of transmuting metals and gemstones. This was the primary purpose of the séances that they held. Interesting but off focus is considered a miss by today's standards of scrying. Kelley's lack of practical results may have been due to him trying to scry something that was not possible in the way that he wanted it to be. This is an important lesson to learn. If you try to scry or dowse something that does not exist, you will get something, and it may even be interesting, but it will not be practical, nor will it be on target.

I believe that Dr. Dee and Kelley did encounter success with their alchemy experiments, though I think what they produced was likely the result of metallic apports rather than transmutation. An *apport* is the teleportation of a small object from one location to another. The energy has to be channeled through a medium, and it is done with a non-corporeal spirit. Kelley was a powerful medium, and I believe that he could have channeled an apport given the right circumstances. I believe in the reality of apports, and have seen them happen on a couple of occasions.

The scrying sessions opened these channels, and for a time Dr. Dee and Kelley were able to succeed. This happened close to the time of the transmission of the Great Table and Enochian calls. I think their success is related to those sessions rather than any content of the communication. I realize the story of their success in alchemy is controversial. I am not here to defend or refute the belief. My purpose in describing their experience is to show how the technique used by Edward Kelley—or, if you prefer, the way the spirits presented the material—helped him scry letters and an unknown language.

The question that should come to mind is "What made the difference between the perception of the Great Table and the earlier tables that basically have not found much practical use over the centuries?" I think I have figured out the key to this mystery.

Kelley, or the spirits working with him, were able to present the material in such a way that his expectation and belief biases were derailed. The Great Table was scrambled and not scryed in its correct order or in such a way that he could figure out the table mentally. It had to be pieced together after the session. The calls were transmitted backward, which again derailed his superficial expectations and biases. By receiving the material in this way, Kelley gives us an example of how to partially hide the target yet still directly scry letters. Let us look at the problem, and the Enochian solution to it.

Numbers can be worked with one only digit at a time. Even double-digit or triple-digit numbers can be dowsed using zero through nine. Letters, on the other hand, are more complex. In the English language we have twenty-six letters, and a few are look-alikes. Lowercase *a*, *o*, and *c*, as well as lowercase *l* and uppercase *I*, are examples of letters that can cause problems scrying because they resemble each other. What is more, letters do not always appear right side up or facing the correct way when they are scryed. They can be inverted or fragmented. It creates a confusing situation. So how do we handle this?

Alphanumeric Hidden Targets

A hidden target containing alphanumerics is one way to address the problem. Letters take practice, and you need to work with inquiries that contain writing before you will develop skill in scrying it. Using, in your target pool, photos of places that contain some letters or writing in the photos is a good way to get a feel for them. Four folded slips of paper with numbers linked to four photos are placed in the grab bag, then one is drawn out and set aside without being opened. The photo linked to the number is scryed for whatever letters it contains, such as street signs, store names on buildings, and so on. You use primary information points just as you do with a regular scrying target. The primary information aspects that letters give are usually *object* or *energy*. You continue from there with the session.

Edward Kelley's first principle of scrying for letters was constant practice. He scryed hundreds, if not thousands, of letters before he developed enough proficiency to scry the Angelic language and the Great Table. He worked on this tirelessly, oftentimes practicing for twelve hours or more per day. He was obsessed with this task, and very determined to be successful.

For the scryer, working a hidden target that contains letters will save quite a bit of time. You will learn this letter scrying faster than Kelley did if you use the grab bag technique for the purpose of dealing with alphanumerics. Scrying a group of photographs that contain letters and numbers, randomly drawn from a target pool, is an efficient way to learn to scry letters. The letters are seen in context at the target site. This makes them easier to scry. I do not know why this is, but it does seem to be easier to get the letters correct if they are in some kind of setting or at an event. Whatever the reason is, the principle is still the same—you need to practice scrying to become good at it. Focused practice on material containing letters is the first principle we learn from Edward Kelley.

Scramble Known Information

The second principle is applicable for working with larger documents and unknown languages. The angels scrambled the information received by Kelley during transmission. The calls were scryed backward. They stopped and started, with significant stretches of time between sessions. This created conditions that made it difficult to bias the information being transmitted.

When you cannot obscure an inquiry, then scramble the information. Break it up. Scry it backward or in random pieces. If you are trying to scry an unknown language or a document written in a language that you cannot read, then you need to scry the information backward. Take extended breaks so that you cannot remember what you did in past sessions.

Divide the unknown document into a grid, labeling each section with a number. Write the numbers representing the sections of the document on folded slips of paper and place them in a grab bag. Draw a number and scry without looking at the number. The section should be small enough to be scryable in a fifteen-minute session.

As you scry, try to discover the letters and the meanings of the letters. This works with hieroglyphic systems, such as ancient Egyptian, and Mesoamerican codices and alphabets that contain imagery that is concrete, such as the ancient Hebrew alphabet, where the letters represent a concept or an object.

Letters will sometimes appear fragmented in the speculum. You need to work quickly and with good focus. Draw what you see, then straighten it out later. If you are working in stealth mode, closed-eyelid scrying works well for this.

With internal scrying, if you know you are going for letters, then you will be fighting bias the whole way through the session. It may be a good idea to mix the alphanumeric inquiries with inquiries that do not have alphanumerics, so that you have a high level of doubt as to whether or not the target contains alphanumerics.

Woo-Woo Targets

If you are scrying an esoteric target such as an alien language or an alien writing system, verification is not possible at the present time. It is a good idea to use that kind of target only after you have gained some proficiency and established accuracy with subjects that are grounded.

It is possible that Edward Kelley, in scrying the Enochian calls, uncovered language of extraterrestrial biological entities. I do not believe the Enochian language he scryed is the language of the spirits called angels in Judeo-Christian mythology. Spirits communicate by telepathy, and usually on a much deeper level than mere language. This is particularly true of higher, more evolved spirits, which would include Judeo-Christian angels. They do not use a verbal or written language.

Because the idea of heaven involves the sky and stars, Dee and Kelley's mental focus when speaking to the Enochian spirits would have been on the heavens. I think it is more likely Kelley picked up an alien language, focused on it, and was able to transmit it at least in part without realizing what it was that was being transmitted. It is possible that the Enochian calls are the transcription of the language of a physical species from another solar system.

When you do a few scrying sessions, you will begin to understand why this is a likely outcome concerning the transmission of the Enochian calls. Only someone who has done scrying can really see how this is possible. Since there is no way to feedback the Enochian language, it is impossible to say how accurate Kelley's work was or where the language came from. I disagree with the theory that the Enochian language was transmitted to Kelley from Dr. Dee via telepathy. I believe there was enough focus in the session to transmit something, and given the understanding of cosmology in the sixteenth century, it seems the most plausible explanation. Nonhuman languages and writing systems are interesting targets and are good for occasional exploration by intrepid scryers. I think that nonhuman languages are a worthy topic for further exploration.

Practice Inquiries

My final advice concerning alphanumerics is to keep these sessions fun to do and not overwork them. It is really easy to burn out doing this kind of target. Burnout creates frustration and anger. Also, I strongly advise you to keep your money safely in your pocket. Betting will introduce expectation bias and will ruin your accuracy rate.

Here are a few easy practice targets for working with alphanumerics:

- High and low temperature of the day
- Average wind speed for the day
- Depth of snowfall in a storm
- Number of hurricanes in a season
- Scores and outcomes of ball games (You can practice this with indirect scrying or dowsing—indirect scrying works very well with the outcomes.)
- Combined scores of ballgames (Add the total number of points earned by each team.)
- Fluctuation of individual stocks and currencies

CHAPTER TWELVE
SYMBOLIC, OCCULT, AND MYSTERY TARGETS

In this chapter I will lay the foundation for scrying symbols for use in various applications including magic, personal growth, spirit communication, and traditional spirit work. Those who have an interest in working with occult systems such as the Enochian calls and tables of Dr. John Dee, the spirits described in the *Steganographia* of the Abbot Johannes Trithemius, and the symbolism of the Tarot and the runes, as well as various forms of spellwork, have a framework that they can use for these highly specialized areas of study.

Even for those who do not have an interest in the occult or systems of magic, there are still important concepts in this chapter that will help with various situations in which you may find yourself. The techniques described here provide an approach for dealing with unverifiable symbolic and occult targets and a way to interpret ambiguous details for verifiable grounded targets.

This is what many of you have been waiting for. I know from experience that when you learn this kind of skill, you have burning questions about the universe that you want answered, and there is no other way to get those answers. There are teachers of psychic arts who discourage this kind of esoteric exploration, but I think it is the greatest motivator there is for doing scrying.

An esoteric target is a target that cannot be validated easily. There is usually very little if any solid information about the target to use for feedback sessions. There are three types of esoteric targets: mystery, symbolic, and occult. So what is the difference between these three types of esoteric targets?

Mystery Targets

A mystery target is an unknown place, event, or entity that has some support for a physical existence. With mystery targets there are usually photos or videos of the object in question that give validation for the scryer. It could also be something that exists but is impossible to verify in your lifetime. Ancient aliens and alien civilizations, cryptozoology, out-of-place artifacts, quantum mechanics, future advanced technologies, and astronomy targets, events, or objects in the distant past are all examples of mystery targets. Completely unknown writings or civilizations about which little is known, such as the Indus Valley, Atlantis, and Lemuria, are all mystery targets. The scryed information about them cannot, at this time, be verified.

There is no reason why a mystery target cannot be hidden and drawn from a grab bag. This should be practiced consistently when working with this kind of target. The procedure with a mystery target does not change from what I have described in the previous chapters. The only difference between a mystery target and a grounded target is the quantity and quality of information available for feedback.

It is always best to be as conservative as possible when doing an interpretation of a mystery target scrying session. When you are doing mystery targets, do not jump immediately to off-world or exotic explanations of the scrying data. Even if you have something clearly exotic or unusual, there is a 30 to 40 percent chance of error in your data if you are average to above-average in your accuracy. Accept the unknown. When I scry mystery targets, I sometimes find that I end up with more questions than answers once I have finished the session and examined and interpreted the results. It is not a bad idea to get a second opinion if the topic is important to you.

Symbolic Targets

Symbols are a part of everyday life and communication. They are present in every culture on Earth. As a scrying target, symbols can be occult or part of a historical or archaeological study. Scrying a symbol gives insight about its true nature and purpose to the seer.

A symbolic target is usually nonphysical and is expressed by a written or astral symbol. The symbol is usually a written symbol. An example of a symbolic target is scrying the astrological symbol of Capricorn. The scryer would look for relationships of the Capricorn symbol and concept to other astrological symbols. Another example of symbolic scrying is scrying the Kabbalistic Tree of Life. Scrying alchemy symbols is yet another symbolic scrying target. The scryer, in doing a symbolic target, is scrying for concepts, ideas, and meaning. Symbolic targets exist as an esoteric concept but are not literal physical or astral places or entities.

When you scry symbols, you look at points of primary information in the same manner as for a grounded, physically based inquiry. However, you know when you do a symbology project that the main aspects will be *energy/activity* and *presence*. When scrying a symbolic system, you still use the primary information points and grab bag system, unless you need a specific setup prescribed by an occult document that you are working with. An example of an occult document would be a grimoire, a ritual such as a Golden Dawn ritual, or an invocation specific to a set of symbols.

It is, however, ideal to hide the target when it is possible to do so. The reason for hiding the target when doing occult symbology is that you can gain new insights into the symbol if you trust your deeper mind and let go of what you consciously know about the symbol. Once you have completed scrying, then you look at the symbol you were working with and discard inaccurate or irrelevant information, keeping the information that is relevant and important. This filtering process adds depth and insight to the properties of the symbol.

Examples of scryable symbols include magic squares, yoga symbols such as the chakras and mandalas, Tarot cards, runes, Enochian spirit sigils, and religious symbols. In addition, objects can also be scryed for symbolic and spiritual content. Symbolic writing systems, such as the hieroglyphics of the ancient Egyptians, or the writing systems of the Mesoamericans are also suitable for symbol scrying. Hebrew is a good alphabet to work with because the letters have associations with various animals and objects of everyday life during ancient times, when the alphabet was created. In glyphic and Hebrew writing, symbolic content is related to the objects, and objects are much easier to work with than the written phonetically-based letter systems. Astrological, occult, and alchemy symbols and charts are really interesting to work with. This method of scrying will add to your knowledge and use of these occult tools.

Mesoamerican writing has not yet been completely translated. Scrying could provide significant insights into that writing system and even produce partial translations of documents that cannot be translated otherwise. Another potentially interesting inquiry might be the astrological features of exoplanetary systems. No exploration of this has been attempted to my knowledge. This would be virgin territory for the adventurous scryer, whose curiosity can range far beyond the bounds of the human physical experience.

For the scryer who is not interested in doing occult symbology, unknown or obscure historical symbols could be scryed for additional information. If you are proficient, you might be able to add to the depth and quality of information regarding a particular writing codex, glyphic works such as cave paintings, or religious symbols such as the Christian cross.

Occult Targets

Symbolic and occult scrying often go hand in hand, and the session and its targets may include both types of scrying. However, occult targets may involve interaction with occult entities such as angels and demons, and lean more toward a mediumship application of scrying skills than symbolic targets do. For symbolic and occult targets, there usually are no physical photos, videos, or other evidence that can validate their existence. It is a matter of belief. Occult targets are documented in ancient magic literature such as the grimoires.

Scrying symbols, occult qualities, and spirits is a basic skill required for the practice of spirit conjuring and magic, which I define as the art of effecting change in the physical world using spiritually based energy. When you are able to scry spirits, you can employ a spirit to do acts of magic, or you can communicate and learn information that is difficult to access or not available any other way. Scrying symbols is a prerequisite for spirit evocation.

Occult scrying was taught and practiced by the Rosicrucian society known as the Hermetic Order of the Golden Dawn, which was founded in London in 1887. It is described in Israel Regardie's book *The Golden Dawn*, which contains the complete teachings of the order. This was first published in four volumes between 1937 and 1940, but there have been other writings that refer to the method, such as Regardie's 1932 book *A Garden of Pomegranates* and Aleister Crowley's work *The Vision and the Voice*, which describes Crowley's experimental scrying of the thirty Enochian Aethyrs in the years 1900 and 1909. Crowley used the method of occult scrying that he learned as a member of the Golden Dawn.

In Regardie's book *The Golden Dawn* (Llewellyn, 6th edition, pp. 458–60), it is recommended to gaze at a symbol, then close your eyes and allow a vision to develop in your mind. Descriptions of encounters with various spirits associated with the symbol and dreamlike visions are the outcome of this technique, and are sought after by the proponents of that particular system of scrying. Occult correspondences are important to the technique, so the scrying is done with conscious knowledge of the target. There is a list of symbols and techniques for testing the spirits you encounter, in order to attempt to eliminate issues with "deception" and bias. Most of these are magical symbols or gestures drawn in the air and the chanting of various divine names or attributes. Generally speaking, the sense of putting it all together or having it "right" is an indication of "deception" or bias starting to kick in, so the use of the occult gestures will be successful only in situations where the seer understands what it feels like when they are off track. The natural tendency will be to go with the superficial mind and belief reinforcement.

Issues with Hiding Symbolic and Occult Targets

The practice of hiding targets first appeared in the parapsychological literature in the nineteenth century. It seems to have started with Dr. Joseph Rodes
Buchanan (1814–1899) around 1840 in the US. Buchanan's *Manual of Psychometry*, which was copyrighted by the author in 1885 and self-published
in 1893, introduced to the general public the hidden target concept with psychometry. A similar technique with even more stringent target hiding was
later used by the Stanford Research Institute in the 1970s, and developed into
a multi-step remote viewing system with various branches. As interest in psychic and spirit phenomena grew, the practice of target hiding also increased in
popularity.

Dr. Buchanan's *Manual of Psychometry* is the earliest reference I could
find to using the obscured target technique for inquiries, and forms the basis
of the internal scrying technique that I teach. Instead of occulted physical
objects, I use statements of intent. This works just as well as an envelope containing a letter or a sack holding an object, both of which Dr. Buchanan used
in his experiments.

As always, I advise hiding targets as much as possible when dealing with
esoteric targets, but I also realize that there are situations in which this cannot be done. There may be times when you need to know what an occult
target is prior to the session, and in those cases the older traditional systems
of scrying work well enough to use. These circumstances may arise when you
need to create a ritual workspace that has colors, objects, incense, and other
physical materials that are compatible with the occult quality or spirit with
which you are working in order to create the right ambience for the session.
However, this is a less than ideal situation, even when such correspondences
must be used in order to do the experiment. Hidden or blind targets are
always best for obtaining accurate results in a scrying session.

It is best to have an established record of accuracy on hidden targets
before attempting to work with front-loading (when information about the
target is known to the scryer prior to the session). The issue of belief bias will
always increase with the increase in knowledge. Attempts to mix up or hide
some of the target information should be made whenever possible. If you
cannot hide the target completely, then at least some of the information that

you are seeking from the spirit or quality present at the target can be made into tasking statements and put into a grab bag. In this way you should be able to identify if you are, in fact, drifting off into a fantasy. Every effort to hide questions and rely completely on Spirit and the deeper mind alone for information is a step in the right direction. When you practice occult scrying, you should always look for ways to work a hidden target into the scrying session.

Challenges with Mystery, Symbolic, and Occult Targets

The initial procedure for scrying symbolic and occult targets is the same that you use for regular scrying targets. If you can do so, hide the symbol by having several other symbols that are completely different in meaning and context in your target pool, and use the grab bag technique. Continue with the square and points of primary information. Since you are looking for context as well as meaning when you mystery scry archaeological symbology, you will need to compare other data against the scryed information.

Occult and symbolic targets have particular challenges that have to be met in order to ensure quality and accuracy and prevent diversion into fantasy or self-deception. The expectation of what the target should represent, or be like, is a challenge. We have called this belief bias. In the case of a non-hidden target, we must deal directly with this challenge. Often our expectations as to when and if the target can be compared to real time and space information are not based in reality. Edward Kelley's transmission of numerous tables, the calls, and other visions is an example of what happens when you cannot eliminate this problem. You get a lot of junk and a little bit of good information that is very difficult to sort out from the garbage.

The reality is that sometimes the target cannot be hidden. When working with a target that has to be scryed in a particular setting with specific tools, you will have to face your bias, which can result in a war in your mind. This is something you must accept. The belief and expectations of your superficial mind will attempt to divert your attention from the deeper-mind data, try to analyze and label it, or obliterate it altogether. You must accept that this will be a polluted session and that you will have to go over the battleground after the fact and pick out the few pieces that appear to be deeper perception from the myriad pieces related to the superficial mind's attempt to hijack the session.

Stick with the Structure

When you attempt to scry a symbolic or occult target that cannot be hidden, you will have prior knowledge, or front-loading. Rather than focusing on the information you know, initiate the session with the square and the three points of primary information. Focus on these primary information aspects instead of the target itself. Adhering to the same structure as that of a grounded session with a hidden target will help you control your mind in such a way that hijacking by the expectation bias of your superficial consciousness will be reduced. You are still looking for descriptions and breaking down the labels into descriptive terms whenever possible.

Because the session structure needs to be maintained, you have to learn the structure to begin with. This is why I suggest doing at least a few sessions with hidden targets to gain proficiency with the general procedure of scrying before even attempting symbolic or occult targets. I am very aware that when most people learn to scry, they want to see things that they do not normally have access to. Most of these motivating targets are mysterious or occult in nature. I accept this, but if you just take a bit of time and learn the structure of the session, you will be able to perceive more accurately and also in greater detail. Once you know that structure, have fun exploring.

The Legend of the Psychic Police

A discussion of ethics is probably desirable as we examine this potent scrying system. The question comes up occasionally, "Can you spy on someone using these techniques?" The answer is, "Yes, you can." There are no protections against this kind of intrusion. Anyone can spy on anyone. Everything in the universe is an open book as far as knowledge is concerned. The only limitations are those you place on yourself, and they are purely personal and psychological in nature.

However, attacking someone using this technique is another matter. Everyone has spirit friends and psychological defenses that will protect them and prevent harm. If you choose to psychically attack someone, you will face reactions to your action. Consequences are unpredictable but inevitable when you engage in aggressive psychic behavior, even if you think it is justified. This includes exorcism. If an entity is causing problems, aggression toward it will raise additional issues. In some cases the additional problems that surface are worth it, especially if the entity is causing extreme distress or physical damage. However, it is always best to try to work a solution that is as gentle, positive, and low-key as possible in these situations.

You are on a level playing field when you engage in scrying and magic. What protects you is basically the same thing that protects other people. Sometimes this energy of protection is personified, and sometimes it is just a quality. There is nothing that will give you an advantage over someone. The protections are natural and usually not something that trigger any kind of conscious awareness. Overt magical aggression, even in defense, usually results in energies that manifest in random and unpredictable ways.

Because the scrying process is passive, there is no energy going out, only an opening up to a particular manifestation or energy. The result is that anything may be observed anywhere and from any time without harmful consequences. This includes extra-dimensional universes. You will not experience any direct consequences from scrying something that is unethical to scry. However, this does not preclude other actions that might be taken against you if the data obtained from the scrying session is published.

A Word about Espionage

Laws against spying, whether it is international, industrial, or personal, will probably apply to scrying if put to the test. I would not tempt legal action by posting or publishing information of a questionable nature. If you publish something you are not supposed to know, there may be attempts to cause you trouble. There may be threats or even lawsuits filed. This can be very expensive even when it does not amount to anything or is not justified. There is always some sort of scandal or dirt going on and being publicized because the news media thrives on gutter talk. Whatever the scandal is, it is not worth your time or effort to bother with. There are far more interesting targets to look at than unctuous politicians or scandalous celebrities with the intelligence and ethics of a city cockroach. I am sorry for insulting cockroaches, but I cannot think of a better analogy at the moment. I suggest putting your valuable time and skills to use elsewhere.

Encountering Entities While Scrying

In esoteric scrying work, you are likely to encounter various entities. This may happen even if it is not your intention. I do not know if these are actual spirits or some kind of shadows created by the mind of the individual. Most of the time the presences are benign or even pleasant.

Though it is rare, it is possible that an entity could attempt to attack you because of scrying. I will say that even though I have experienced a few rare attacks, it is usually a bluff of appearance, and once the illusion is defeated, the attack ends. The effect is entirely illusionary. The passive nature of scrying will not provoke reactions that do anything more than startle. It has no more possibility of creating physical harm than a bad dream does. The response of the seer should be just like responding to a bad dream. You say, "Oh, it's just a dream," and let it go. At that point the episode ends and you can continue.

I believe this is defensive behavior on the part of natural telepaths or spirits. It could also be a fear reaction to your presence, which the entity might consider to be alien. I do not believe that humans are the only entities in this universe that have this kind of reaction to an alien entity. It may also be a reflection of your reaction of fear to an entity alien to you, and that reflection is your psychological defense designed to make you back off. I think the latter is the most likely explanation. When anyone has asked me about an attack related to scrying, this has almost always been the cause of the perception.

Once you back down out of the scrying session, then the problem usually subsides. I have only had this issue arise with occult grimoire-type spirits. In retrospect I think it was a result of confusion, and because many of these spirits are shadows intentionally created as servitors, they retain some of the emotional characteristics of human beings.

There have been reports by people who intentionally remote-viewed (CRV) aliens or alien vehicles that the aliens seemed to be aware of them as they were doing the session. A notable example is in the book *Penetration* by Ingo Swann. This is not the only incident that I am aware of. Most of the time, the aliens' response is one of being startled; then, once they realize what is going on, they calm down and usually ignore the presence. I had a situation where they responded with curiosity. It led to some weird but harmless experiences. I have never run into any situations where an alien entity caused harm. Perhaps we cause them to have some weird experiences, too.

Alternative Feedback Techniques

Feedback is a challenging issue when scrying subjects that are completely unknown. There are some alternatives to traditional feedback that the scryer can utilize. These strategies do not replace traditional feedback, but they can assist the scryer in situations where there is little to no information available on the target. The alternatives should be used to slow down the deterioration of the scryer's accuracy that occurs when scrying without proper feedback.

One method of working with such inquiries is to have multiple seers on one project. The symbol is selected at random, and the group works together. Various individuals scry the object while one who is not a scryer compiles the information.

If the scryer is working with a group, it is a common practice to use what is called consensus feedback. This is when the data of the various sessions are compiled and the perceptions that show up on more than one session are seen as a consensus. The individuals then judge their sessions on the perceptions seen most commonly in the group. The feedback is the compilation of information rather than the actual physical characteristics of the target. This is not a perfect way of doing feedback, but it is better than no feedback. The accuracy in these groups usually runs around 60 percent. It is not a definitive way of scrying a symbol that is unknown. However, even with a 30 to 40 percent margin of error, a group working together has the potential to uncover insights into an unknown document or symbol where there are no other alternatives.

The second alternative feedback technique that is helpful for the solitary scryer is doing multiple sessions on the same target. The target is placed back into the grab bag for additional sessions. When additional sessions are done, look for consensus between the sessions. The perceptions that agree with each other have a greater chance of being correct.

I would suggest that a 60 percent hit rate on grounded inquiries be established by the scryer before attempting to do this kind of work. I do not mean you have to practice for years before scrying unknown artifacts, but you do need to understand where your strong points and weak points are when you scry. You need a confident sense of how accurate you are on known targets before you try for one that is not known. Before trying to translate a document that has not yet been translated, work with one that has a known translation and see how well the procedure, which I will outline next, works for you.

Procedure for Scrying Symbols

Scrying symbols is an interesting and meaningful scrying project. A symbol is an ideogram that represents an idea or a concept that is often abstract and difficult to express in verbal terms. It is a visually expressed idea. A well-known example of a symbol is the Wiccan pentagram.

Symbols are common in established religions. Scrying can uncover deeper aspects to the meaning, origins, and history of the use of symbols. Scrying a symbol is not all that different from scrying any other target. You start with a grab bag and proceed with the session much in the same way you would with a physical target.

Step One: The Grab Bag

If you can use a grab bag, place the paper slips describing the symbols that are your targets into their own separate grab bag. It is best not to mix up symbolic scrying with inquiries that involve places, events, entities, or objects. If you are working with objects that have ritual symbolism, these should also be separated into their own target pool. Symbols in the bag can be from different systems. For example, if you want to examine the meaning of Tarot cards and runes, you can put slips for those in the same grab bag. In fact, it is probably a good idea to do so, since it increases the level of doubt as to what you drew out of the bag. Anything that reduces guessing is helpful.

Step Two: The Target

Select your folded paper slip and set it aside without looking at it. If you have a target that is not hidden, write the tasking on a slip of paper and set it aside.

This is the same as if you were doing a grab bag target. You do not have to hide the tasking statement, but set it out of sight while you are scrying so you can focus on the points of primary information.

Step Three: Points of Primary Information

This is the exact same procedure you learned in chapter 1. Stay with this procedure even if you are working with a known target. Do not focus on the target, but instead draw your square box and set down your three dots. Find the points of primary information for each dot just as you have been doing up to this point.

Step Four: Do Your Scrying Session

You now have several scrying techniques to use. Use one or more to describe the aspects of primary information. You are not directly scrying the target, but instead the points of primary information, just as you would with a hidden target. If you can work with a hidden target, it is of course much better. In addition to your scrying session, you may want to add the following targeting questions if you are working with symbols. If you are working with an occult target, you can add these questions at your discretion if you feel they are applicable.

A. How does this symbol change the feel of the room?
B. How does this symbol feel? What kind of emotional energy is it emitting?
C. How does this symbol feel esoterically?
D. How does this symbol make you feel? How do you react emotionally to the symbol?
E. How do you react spiritually to this symbol? How does this symbol change you?

Remember, you are not guessing what the symbol is; you are deciphering the energy it puts out. Picture the square with the symbol in it but covered up. You do not yet know what that symbol is. However, that symbol radiates energy, and even though it is covered up, it will change the atmosphere, the feeling of the paper, and the area around it. How that symbol feels as you probe it with your pen or pencil will reveal something about its meaning.

Step Five: Interpreting Primary Information for Symbolic Scrying

Spiritual or esoteric reactions can be related to elemental and astrological factors. If you are familiar with the four ancient elements and with the energies of the planets and zodiac signs of astrology, you can use these factors to help you describe changes in the spiritual energy of the room and in yourself as you explore the symbol. For example, fire as an element is hot, dry, active, impulsive, and sometimes destructive. Water is cold, wet, flowing, intuitive, dark, or dimly luminescent. The zodiac sign Scorpio is sexual, dark, piercing, and active. And so on. Using these elemental and astrological factors will help give you a base from which to work through the descriptions of the perceptions you get when you scry a symbol.

Summary

Scrying esoteric targets, which include symbolic, occult, and mystery targets, is often a big motivator for learning the art of scrying. I encourage exploration of topics of interest to keep the scrying fresh and fun. Bear in mind that overdoing these kinds of targets will cause a deterioration of skills and accuracy. Feedback is the only way to improve your scrying and prevent deterioration. It is the key to perfecting the art. If it is not available because of the nature of the target, then a couple of alternatives have been given. These are not substitutes for physically based information for the feedback session.

These kinds of targets lay the groundwork for doing magic and spirit conjuration. The practices of working that I have described are also useful for active magical work. Feedback, consistency, and structure all play a vital role in working with talismans, amulets, spells, spirits, and inner alchemy. Learning to use this structure now will help you later on when you advance to active magic by giving you an effective and powerful framework upon which to build additional skills.

CHAPTER THIRTEEN
THE LIGHTHOUSE RITUAL

In this chapter I am going to introduce you to a ritual that has helped me over the past few years as I was learning not only how to scry but how to do so accurately. The Lighthouse Ritual is the most unique, and in many ways the most important, component of the method of scrying taught in this book. It relies upon the ability of precognition to transcend the barriers not only of space but also of time. By incorporating this ritual into your scrying practice, you enable your future self to communicate information to your past self, and in this way convey to you knowledge of events that have not yet occurred. It is an essential tool if you are scrying such things as future sports events, stock market trends, or lottery numbers. Its correct use will dramatically enhance the accuracy of your predictions, particularly when doing alphanumeric scrying, which is a challenge for most scryers. Alphanumeric scrying can be very useful for lotteries and financial targets, as well as for deciphering the writing on artifacts where an unknown lettering system was used.

The Lighthouse Ritual is done both prior to beginning scrying and after the feedback session has been completed. The basic structure of the session—obtaining the primary information points, the process of scrying, and the feedback session—must be practiced and learned first before attempting to incorporate the Lighthouse Ritual. When the session structure has been memorized and the scryer feels comfortable with using it, then the Lighthouse Ritual may be added to it.

This ritual gives additional filtering to help the scryer become more accurate. Once it is started, it is an ongoing ritual that takes a couple of months of regular practice before it reaches its peak effect. If the regular use of the ritual is interrupted, it will require time to rebuild the effectiveness of it. The Lighthouse Ritual is not scrying in and of itself. It provides a kind of feedback loop that filters the information the scryer perceives during the session. Its regular use gradually increases the accuracy of that information. While the ritual is not scrying, it does utilize the information you obtained in the feedback part of the scrying session. So it is important for the ritual that all parts of the scrying session be done, including the feedback session.

I measured the ritual's effectiveness initially by participating in a study group that attempted to predict gaming and financial outcomes and changes. The group as a whole was not doing the ritual, but I was using the ritual on my personal projects that I turned in for the group's predictions. On financial targets, my hit rate went from 60 percent to 90 percent over a period of a couple of months. The only technique changed during that time was the Lighthouse Ritual. Hit rates do fluctuate, and my rate would peak and drop. The average over time rose a few percentage points, from 65 percent to 69 percent over the space of eight months. The effect of the ritual is still considered to be significant, as it did measurably improve my baseline accuracy. After this study, I was convinced that the Lighthouse Ritual is a powerful tool for increasing accuracy.

The object of the ritual is to create what I call a quantum time loop. In this time loop, you essentially change the past from a point of time in the future. The scrying session is always in the present, and in that sense is the center point between the past and the future, so you create changes in focus prior to the scrying session. You make the changes according to information you obtain in the future when you evaluate the session's accuracy. This time loop can be formed over the span of a month or two, if sessions are done weekly. The loop affects the past from the future, with the static midpoint maintained at the time of the scrying session. In order to establish the time loop, the inquiry that the scryer is working on must be verifiable in time and space.

You can also create this loop by making mental contact with your past and future selves. When I practice this directly, I visualize a tunnel going to the past or to the future, depending on which part of the ritual I am working. Another method is to use the higher self or your spirit guide. Sometimes it is easier to visualize a messenger spirit of some kind going back and forth along your timeline. The ritual is abstract and focuses on time in a different way than we usually understand it. The cultural belief that the past cannot be changed is a major challenge for comprehending and working with this ritual. Conceptualization of the time loop is easier if you have a messenger and employ an entity that you believe is capable of going to the past and the future without difficulty. In most cases, the spirit will be the scryer's spirit guide or higher self. If you have issues with belief in spirits, do this directly with your own mind. It is a mental reaching out to your future and past selves.

For a beginner, it is easiest to initiate the ritual with a few simple tools. This is done with the understanding that once you know how to do the ritual, you will phase out its material aspects and work solely with mental focus and visualization. If you want to use a spirit, the mental focus is on sending that messenger back and forth through time. If you cannot use tools because of privacy issues, you can still do the ritual. It may take a bit longer to get the loop established. You can also change the tools, as long as you keep the ritual itself intact. I will describe some of the tools next.

The Altar

As much as possible, the altar needs to be your own design. I would recommend that all the tools you use for the Lighthouse Ritual be separate from anything else that you might use. The setup can be made simple or complex, depending on your own personal inclinations. It also depends on your location and the situation that exists when you are working. Once you have started the ritual, you should continue it regularly. Discarding the tools should be done over time as you learn how the ritual feels and gain the ability to picture it in your mind.

For visualization, I suggest that either sketches of an altar or an actual physical altar be made at home. It is easier to visualize something if it exists in material reality. The altar can be small, even as small as eight-by-eight inches on its square top. The altar may need to remain in place for a long time, depending on how long it takes for the feedback of the scrying session to be studied. The altar and supplies are called *materia magica*, a common term for any items used in magic.

Tools on the Altar

I recommend two items for the center of focus of the altar: a candle and an incense burner. For my altar, I use a candle that is held by a brass angel. I do not "dress" the candle because of fire hazard. Dressing a candle is a practice used in candle magic of coating a candle with oil. I've had a few dressed candles flame up on me, so I make sure that I do not have to be concerned with that. The candle has to be replaced periodically. I use the same type of candle throughout the Lighthouse Ritual working.

For the incense, I always make my own. I dry herbs that I grow myself for the most part. For this work I burn mugwort, which has a consensus association with psychic work. I make a bundle of herbs that have been dried for the ritual: cedar, mugwort, and a sea grass that smells sweet when burned. I smoke the herbs for thirty seconds or less per session. I do not burn the material through the entire session. It is very bad for the respiratory system to do this. Also, I find it distracting to work in a smoky room if I perform the ritual indoors. I associate this particular odor with the ritual and only use this combination of herbs for the Lighthouse Ritual. The candleholder is only used for this working as well.

Visualizing the Altar

You do not have to be physically at the altar to use it. When you have the candle and incense set up, you need to hold the image in your mind of the altar, candle, and incense. While thinking of how they look, sound, and smell, practice lighting the candle and studying the flame. You should be able to picture this in your mind when you are away from the altar. The smell of the herbs when they are smoking is the other visualization that you need to be able to recall in your mind when you work away from the altar. If you practice this at home a few times, it will be easier to do when you are away.

Spiritual Protection

If you are afraid of scrying, that fear needs to be addressed before you start working. It is important to understand that you can generate hazards when you are fearful and feel the need for protection. A safe feeling should be present to the point where you do not worry about creating talismanic safeguards. Nothing can harm you unless you generate the opening with your belief that this can happen. There are no physical manifestations that can occur when scrying unless you channel them. You are in charge of your energy and the spiritual forces you experience.

That being said, the following things can be done to help you control the energies within your space. For the Lighthouse Ritual away from the altar, you can do these mentally in stealth mode without moving physically. The circle is the area of focus of your ritual, and it is your safe space. It does not have to be large. It can be as small as your head.

To Create a Mental Working Space

In the ritual prior to starting, clear your mind, and with a light coming from your heart, clear and brighten up the area around you. Make a sphere of this brightness that is programmed to stay there while you scry. Nothing can enter this sphere except you and your higher self or guide. Once you have visualized it, trust that it stays there while your attention is on scrying. So you mentally create a working place in your mind that is exclusive to all but you and your guide and that will remain there until you are finished. It stays there regardless of where you place your focus when you are working. All you have to do is imagine it and fix it into place.

At home you can practice ritual circles, smudging, and other more complex ritual procedures to prevent unwanted intrusion into the session. I do not do these kinds of procedures myself, but I understand that others may not feel very safe or secure if they do not. I prefer to keep things simple. My sphere and the light are created instantly. The circle does not have to be physical as long as you have a good mental image of what it looks like. *Tarot*

Magic by Donald Tyson (Llewellyn, 2018) is a good resource to read for this kind of work.

Time Loop Initiation

Because this ritual is a time loop ritual, at some point you need to start to initiate the quantum loop. This loop is not a one-time thing. The effect of the Lighthouse Ritual is cumulative. It takes a couple of months to bring it to full strength. This is why it's important to be consistent in practicing it. It does not work as a one-shot deal.

You must be clear about what you are doing in this ritual. It's a bit hard to wrap your mind around it at first because we are so used to linear thinking, which always moves from the past to the future. This ritual has two parts. The perceptive part takes place in the present and the projective part in the future. Or, if you look at it another way, the projective part takes place in the present and the perceptive part in the past. When you are working the projective part, it is your present and you are projecting a message into your past; but when you are working the perceptive part, it is your present and you are receiving a message from your future. It's trippy, I know, but if you think about it, you will understand what is going on.

Initiate this ritual for the first time at the end of a scrying session. The loop must be initiated with a subject of inquiry that is grounded and verifiable. If the target (subject of inquiry) is precognitive, then the time span between the session and the results needs to be short the first time you do the ritual—within a day or so of the scrying, and no more than a week. This ritual has to start immediately after feedback is obtained for the scrying session. Once you have started the loop, then it is continuous and must be sustained.

The projective part of the Lighthouse Ritual done in the future always relates to the perceptive part completed in the past. Each scrying target has its own separate Lighthouse Ritual. Multiple sessions and several months may elapse between the two parts of a ritual. You must keep careful notes to ensure that the future projective part of each ritual is connected with the correct perceptive part of the past. You may be running several rituals at a time if you are working with multiple scrying targets. As you work with this, it does get easier and more natural. By the time you have proficiency, multiple rituals will not be a problem.

Example of the Lighthouse Ritual

For an example, say I am scrying in January to make a prediction about who will win the Super Bowl, which is played in the following month. You will use the associative scrying method to determine your prediction for this kind of target. I do the session, reveal the photos for the prediction, and match the session data to determine which photo represents the prediction to be made. Because the subject of inquiry is precognitive, I have only partial feedback immediately after the session when I look at the tasking statement, which informs me what the subject of inquiry was. The final feedback will happen in February, when a team wins the Super Bowl. After the game has been played, the outcome is known, and the session feedback is available, the Lighthouse Ritual will start.

Projective Part of the Ritual

At this point you have written down the results of your prior session and the actual outcome of the event. In doing an event prediction, it is important that you be very black-and-white in your assessment. The prediction should be written on your paper on a line, then the physical outcome or result on the following line, with the discrepancies noted and clearly visible. If you waffle and try to interpret your work to fit the outcome, there will be no improvement in future scrying sessions, and there is a likelihood of a gradual deterioration of accuracy. You must be very strict about this.

You will not be 100 percent accurate. Most predictions in the work I participate in have about a 55 to 60 percent accuracy rate in the long term. This does fluctuate. There are times when you will not be accurate and times when you can hit over 90 percent. Do not become emotionally attached to this. When you work alone, it is very important to be as objective as possible. So now for each piece of data from the session, you have written below it the actual result from your feedback. Complete the following steps to work the ritual.

1. Write the feedback on a small strip of paper. Only a few words to represent what is written on your page are needed. The strip of paper should be as small as possible.

2. Light or visualize the candle burning on your altar. Ignite and burn the herbs or incense for a few seconds to generate a small amount of fragrant smoke, or visualize the smell and appearance of the smoke in your mind.

3. Mentally focus on the date of your scrying session of this target. Remember yourself sitting at a desk, in the circle, or wherever the session occurred. Feel yourself there, scrying and writing. Move to the moments when you scryed and wrote down the perceptions you had.

4. Take the small strip of paper and carefully burn it in the candle flame. Send a message to yourself in that session, in the past, as to what the final result was—*was*, rather than *will be*, because for you the result has already happened and you know it with absolute certainty. Blow through the smoke of the burning strip and the smoke of the incense as a message to your past self in that session. You may wish to murmur the message you wrote on the strip of paper as you do this. If you cannot burn the paper, then visualize the message floating to your past self, riding on the scent of your incense. If you employ a spirit messenger to assist you, then blow the smoke to the spirit, who then takes the message to your past self doing the session. The elements of the smoke and light of the flame with the message are what the spirit will carry across time and space to the past.

5. Extinguish the candle and the incense, physically or mentally, depending on your circumstances.

This ritual should be performed after feedback is obtained for every session you do from now on. If you break this discipline, the loop will have to be rebuilt and you will have a period of less accurate sessions. Connecting to that previous session where you obtained the data is important. You need to feel and intensely visualize yourself there. Be with yourself in that past session as you are working. Now the loop is initiated.

Receptive Part of the Ritual

The second, receptive part of the ritual starts when you are initiating a scrying session. It actually takes place earlier in time than the first, projective part. You have everything out and ready to go. This ritual is done just prior to the scrying. These elements can be done physically or mentally. If you have trouble doing them in your imagination, practice the ritual physically a few times to get it set in your mind.

1. Light the candle on the altar. Ignite your incense and allow it to burn briefly.
2. Focus your mind on the future where you have done the feedback session and are doing the Lighthouse Ritual at the end of that session. At that point in the future, your future self is sending your present self a message as you sit at the table and look at the candle. The message's purpose is to inform your present self about the results of the scrying session. Receive that message.
3. Breathe in the scent of the incense, and let it carry the message from the future to you.
4. Extinguish your candle and incense.

The Loop

In the feedback session, you are projecting a message to your past self. Prior to scrying, you are perceiving that message from your future self. Now before the scrying session starts, connect to your future and channel the information you are seeking in the scrying session. Spend a few minutes making this connection and opening to your future self or your messenger spirit. Once the connection is made, extinguish the candle. The smoke from the incense represents that information still hanging about in the area. This influences your scrying to direct the energies toward the desired results and give accurate information.

After the scrying is completed, write down each piece of data and the time that the feedback session needs to be done. For long-term readings, make sure the feedback session is marked on a calendar so you will not forget to do it.

Lighthouse Ritual on the Road

This is an alternative ritual you can use if you are doing sessions completely away from home. If you travel or have a situation where you have limited space or privacy, such as a job site, this may work better for you. Also, if you have trouble doing the ritual mentally, this alternative will add physical components that are easier to work with than a strictly mental exercise. The ritual needs to be consistent. Once you start this, you need to keep things rolling the same way.

You don't want to burn paper, candles, and incense in a motel room or at work, right? Not unless you want someone in uniform showing up asking why the smoke alarm went off. So what can you use in a situation with limited space and privacy?

Here's what you can do. First, you need a couple of little things. You need a tealight LED bulb. It is like a fake candle. It is small, the size of a tealight. For smoke you can use a small container with a scent in it like incense. What I would suggest is to melt a bit of soft wax and use an essential oil or combination of oils in it and let it harden in a small container. This way it won't make a mess and can be reused. If the scent starts to fade, then scratch off the top layer of wax and the scent will be renewed. The tart burners for making a pleasant scent in the house are perfect for this. These are small pots of wax that are melted to release a scent. You just keep the wax in a small closed container, opening it only when you do the ritual. The scent will last quite a long time. A subtle, inoffensive scent is best for this, so you don't draw attention from people around you.

When you start with a scent, it is helpful to continue using the same one. Do not switch aspects of the ritual around. If you do change parts of the operation, it will take some time to reestablish the association. Do not use the scent for anything else but the Lighthouse Ritual. When you finish a session, write down the results briefly in your notebook. Light your "candle" and blow the scent when you open the container to your past self doing the scrying session. You inhale the scent and receive the message associated with it if you are receiving information from your future self. You do not have to burn the paper containing the results—instead, you can keep the paper in a notebook and use the scent to carry the message. A spirit can be employed to help with this if you wish. The spirit is visualized carrying the message written on the paper, both the spirit and the paper are covered in scent, and the spirit holds the light of the LED fake candle in its hand.

Four General Rules to Follow

Here are four helpful rules to make the Lighthouse Ritual most effective.

Rule One

When do you begin this ritual, it must be done every time you scry. It should be incorporated into your scrying sessions. The ritual has a cumulative effect. If you do not build up and maintain this effect, then performing the ritual will be worthless. This is the true nature of spellwork and magic. One-shot deals are rarely effective. The work has to be consistent in order for the time loop to be established and stabilized.

Rationale: There is a quantum time loop generated by this ritual. Every moment in time leads to potential events both past and present. You have to generate and maintain that time loop.

Rule Two

Generation of the time loop needs to be performed consistently. Always work the ritual in the same way with the same tools.

Rationale: We are dealing with subtle and sensitive energies. I found out through trial and error that if the ritual is varied, the results will change. The time loop that you generate through this ritual is best reinforced by following a pattern. If you understand the concept of magical streams—that a consistent performance will yield consistent results—you will understand why this is the best practice to follow.

Rule Three

Your focus has to be both conscious and subconscious for the ritual to be effective.

Rationale: Strong, clear focus is essential to the integrity of the ritual. Any distraction will diminish the effect. It is said that magic is accomplished by belief, focus, and intent. These are not sufficient to affect the baseline psychic or magical ability. Belief is actually not required beyond the point of having a willingness to follow the structure provided. Focus has to be directed specifically in order to provide a positive effect, which is what the ritual does. If you are consciously very desirous of the result and emotionally involved with it, the subtle spiritual energies will be overwhelmed and you will lose your connection to Spirit. Intent should be emotionally neutral and only enough to motivate you to do the ritual and the reading work. Patient persistence is a better way to describe the feeling of intent that is effective. Something emotional, like lust or greed, is detrimental and will cause a break in the connection to the subtle perceptions. Without that connection, you are left with mere physical effort and cannot effect any kind of change using spiritual energies.

Rule Four

In order to do this ritual effectively, careful documentation must be kept. The date of the psychic reading or the séance, and the information obtained during these sessions, must be written down accurately and precisely. I keep a notebook of long-term sessions or important sessions that might become lost should the electronic formats fail or become outdated.

Rationale: Documentation is essential to keep track of the loop. You have to be able to focus on the period of time when you performed the ritual, regardless of the timing of the feedback. Feedback usually occurs immediately after the scrying session when the target is revealed, but sometimes, when doing predictions, feedback might not be done for months or even years after the session or séance takes place. In order for this ritual to work, it must be performed consistently, regardless of the time span involved. It is also essential to the structure of the ritual that information obtained in the scrying session be recorded precisely. It is unlikely that the medium or psychic would remember the information needed to perform the ritual months later if it were not written down, so it is important to keep very accurate records once the loop is initiated.

CONCLUSION

I hope that in this book you have found something useful and practical. I have updated older methods of scrying and developed more efficient ways to work in situations where limited time is available and there are less than ideal conditions as far as privacy and space are concerned. The technique presented is secular, but it can be used in spiritual ritual settings. It can also be used by those who do not have any particular spiritual inclinations. Scrying is a natural ability that all humans and some other earthly creatures possess. It allows you to connect to a deeper source of information and spirituality, regardless of how that spirituality appears to you.

GLOSSARY

alphanumeric scrying: The scrying of numbers or letters.

ARV (associative remote viewing): Determining the outcome of a binary question by remote-viewing one of two images that are associated with the target.

aspects: See *primary information.*

aura scrying: An aura is a layer of colored light surrounding the human body that is perceptible to some scryers. Different colors and patterns in the aura indicate emotional states and physical health. Aura scrying is a type of environmental scrying.

bias: An existing bias concerning the target being scryed or dowsed will result in a faulty perception of the data. The bias in the conscious mind overwhelms the faint stream of information rising from the deeper mind during scrying. This bias can take several forms. Belief bias is a learned belief regarding a target. Expectation bias is the prior anticipation of a certain result. Confirmation bias occurs when a result validates your prior assumptions. All forms of bias are destructive to scrying accuracy.

binary dowsing: A method of dowsing used to determine the answers to questions that can only be answered in one of two opposite ways. These include yes-no questions, greater-lesser, higher-lower, and so on.

blind target: A blind target is slightly different from a hidden target. A hidden target is where you set up your own target pool and randomly select your target without looking at it. A blind target is where a task manager— someone who is not scrying the target—sets up the target pool. When using a hidden target, you know what goes into the pool, but not which specific target you are scrying in each session. When using a blind target, you don't even know what went into the pool.

branching a session: When you use different points of view when scrying to obtain more than one perspective on a question, it is known as branching the scrying session.

casting: A form of scrying where you study different materials and look for patterns in them related to the aspects of primary information.

channeling: Spirit communication by means of a medium.

consensus feedback: This occurs when the generally accepted meaning of a target that is viewed by multiple scryers is what constitutes the criteria against which the scrying session is examined.

CRV (controlled remote viewing): A complex seven-step process used to describe a target.

cryptid: An animal that is alleged to exist but not officially recognized.

deeper mind: The aspect of mind that is beneath or beyond consciousness. It is from this mysterious region of the mind that psychic perceptions arise.

dot matrix dowsing: A dowsing technique in which a random number of dots are tapped into a square drawn on a sheet of paper using a pencil. The square is divided into four parts. An even number of dots counted over the entire square is a "yes" response, while an odd number of dots in the total square is a "no" response. However, if two of the sub-squares have an even number of dots and two have an odd number of dots, the answer may be interpreted as weak or uncertain.

dowsing: A method for psychically locating things that are concealed. Traditionally, dowsing has been used most commonly to discover veins of metal ore or water beneath the ground, to determine the location for a mine or well. The dowser will often use metal rods, a wooden wand, or a pendulum, but none of these aids are essential.

dowsing chart: A graphical arrangement of zones that relate to various values. For example, a pie chart could be used for a dowsing chart.

dowsing divisional square: A square drawn on a map that represents the area of the map to be dowsed.

entities: Nonhuman, self-aware beings who may be corporeal or noncorporeal, such as aliens, angels, and spirits.

environmental scrying: The practice of detecting a faint shimmer in the air above scrying targets that are buried or otherwise hidden from view; also, the perception of shapes in complex environmental patterns, such as those that occur in trees, grass, etc.

esoteric target: Targets that are not tangible or are not verifiable are classed as esoteric targets. There are three types of esoteric targets: mystery, symbolic, and occult.

evocation: The practice in magic of calling spirits forth to visible appearance so that they can be communicated with and instructed to perform tasks.

exoplanets: Planets that lie beyond the limits of our solar system.

expectation: A sense that a certain result will or must occur during scrying. It creates a bias in the conscious mind that inhibits the link with the deeper mind and causes unreliable perception of the data.

external scrying: Scrying with the aid of physical tools, such as a mirror, a crystal ball, and so on.

fantasy: When bias in the conscious mind causes the scryer to construct a story line or narrative to explain the scrying data, it is called a fantasy. These story lines are almost always false.

feedback: The evaluation of scrying data against known information about the target is referred to as doing feedback. When a group of scryers scry a single target, the data they agree upon is called the consensus feedback. Regular feedback is factual data, while consensus feedback is conjectural data arrived at by consensus.

field dowsing: When a dowser physically moves through the setting in which they are trying to locate an item, it is called field dowsing.

forced response: The deliberate induction of movement in the dowsing pendulum, in contrast to the natural dowsing response, which does not need to be deliberately induced.

front-loading: A term used in remote viewing when viewing a target that is known. Remote viewers prefer to have no prior knowledge of the target.

grab bag: A bag used to hold a collection of hidden targets, from which one is selected for scrying without its content being revealed.

gray area dowsing: A method of dowsing to answer questions that have a range of possible responses, rather than a simple yes-no response, as in binary dowsing.

grounded target: A scrying target with a high level of verifiable information.

group scrying: When a team of scryers scrys a single target and correlates their perceptions.

hidden target: A hidden target is a target chosen by the scryer prior to the scrying session, along with many other targets, to make up a target pool, but is not specifically known to the scryer during the particular session in which it is the target. It should not be confused with a blind target, which is selected by someone other than the scryer and is completely unknown to the scryer.

ideomotor effect: Meaningful and informative coordinated body movements that are beyond the control of the conscious awareness. The movement of a Ouija board pointer is one example; automatic writing is another. The source of these movements is presumed to be either the deeper mind or external spirit intelligences.

inquiries: An inquiry is the target of the scrying session. There are several types of inquiry. A tangible inquiry is a space-time target about which information is known or will be known. A partially tangible target has some information that will not be known. An esoteric target is nonphysically based or one that has no verifiable characteristics.

internal scrying: A scrying technique that uses only the imagination, with no external tools.

internal symbolism: When the analytical mind translates perceptions arising from the deeper mind into explicit symbols, such as "tree," "house," or "dog."

invocation: The practice in magic of calling spirits into oneself in order to experience their natures and control their forces, or of calling spirits into objects such as statues or rings.

knowledge burden: Prior knowledge of some aspect or aspects of a hidden target. A knowledge burden tends to encourage expectation bias.

labels: Nouns are labels. When an explicit person, place, or thing arises in the mind during scrying, it is called a label. Such things as "tree," "house," or "dog" are labels. They usually are the result of expectation bias or confirmation bias, and should not be accepted at face value, but should be set aside to be broken down into their component parts for later analysis.

Lighthouse Ritual: A technique that utilizes a quantum time loop to increase accuracy in scrying and dowsing. The ritual is done in two parts: a receptive part that takes place just before a target is scryed, and a projective part that is done after information about the target has been verified in a feedback session. In this way, a loop of information is created from the future to the past, which informs the scryer concerning the outcome of the prediction or nature of the target.

magic: The art of effecting change in the physical world using spiritually based energy.

magical stream: A type of magic that relies on a particular set of beliefs or practices; a term used in chaos magic.

mala beads: Buddhist prayer beads, used in a way that is similar to the use of a rosary by Roman Catholics.

materia magica: The physical materials used in a magical working or ritual are called *materia magica.*

meditation: A method of stilling the thoughts and quieting the mind. It has little value in scrying, apart from teaching the scryer how to sit without moving when scrying with a speculum.

mystery target: A mystery target is a target that may or may not have a physical reality. See *esoteric target.*

number line: A line segment drawn on paper to indicate a range of numbers. One end of the line indicates the low end of the range, and the other end indicates the high end. It is used in gray area dowsing.

object: One of the four aspects of primary information that provide initial insight and direction when scrying.

obscured target: A target of the scrying session not known to the seer. Both blind targets and hidden targets are obscured targets.

occult target: A type of esoteric target related to occult symbols, entities, or other characteristics.

oppositional dowsing: This occurs when you dowse not the correct response you are seeking but the exact opposite of that response.

partially tangible targets: Targets that have both verifiable and unverifiable components.

points: The four aspects of primary scrying information are accessed by setting down three dots, or points, in a triangular pattern inside a square. Touching a point enables perception of one or more of these four aspects of information, and serves to focus and direct subsequent scrying of the question.

primary information: The primary information aspects are four general categories of information that are scryed in order to obtain a structure to follow when doing a subsequent, more detailed scrying of the target. The four categories are *object, presence, liquid,* and *energy/activity.*

psychic police: Spiritual entities who are conjectured to control and suppress psychic activities.

psychometry: Psychic perception of information associated with objects that is acquired by means of physical touch. Also, an internal sensing of information that does not rely on seeing or hearing.

quantum time loop: Knowledge gained in the future by conventional methods is fed back into the past to be scryed. The quantum time loop is the underlying mechanism of the Lighthouse Ritual.

remote viewing: A form of scrying developed by a team of scryers working for the US military during the final quarter of the twentieth century.

retinal fatigue: The fatigue that occurs in the eyes when you stare at something for a long time without moving your eyes or blinking. It typically takes the form of a blackness or shadow closing around or covering your field of vision.

scrying: A mode of perception that does not rely on the physical senses. Scrying usually takes a visual form. Even though sight is not required for scrying, the scryed information is usually in the form of shapes, colors, images, or scenes. There are two kinds of scrying: internal and external.

seer: A scryer, particularly someone who uses scrying to make predictions or give prophecy about the future. Nostradamus was a seer.

session: The process of scrying a target. It may be single or multiple. A multiple session is when you scry the same target more than once in order to gain additional information about it.

sigils: Symbolic designs that represent the identities of spiritual beings or magical tasks.

smudging: This is the practice of burning herbs or incense to make an aromatic smoke believed to have cleansing, healing, attractive, or repellent power.

speculum: A tool used for scrying at which the scryer gazes. Common speculums are crystal balls, mirrors, basins of water, and other transparent or reflective objects.

Spirit: The divine essence that pervades the universe and animates living organisms. In this book it is capitalized as Spirit to distinguish it from spirits, which are intelligent, noncorporeal entities such as angels.

statement of intent: A command statement for your subconscious that tells your deeper mind where to go and what to look at. When written down on a slip of paper and put into the grab bag, it becomes a tasking statement.

stealth scrying: Methods for scrying in a public place where you wish to avoid notice. An example of stealth scrying would be when you scry into your mug of coffee or cup of tea at a restaurant.

subject of inquiry: A general statement of the topic you wish to scry. This may be broken down into multiple specific statements of intent, placed in the grab bag as tasking statements.

synchronicity: A concept originated by Carl Jung, who believed that two or more events could be meaningfully related without being causally related. Most people would set this down to chance or luck, but Jung maintained that the meaningful relationship was not accidental.

tapping: A dowsing technique that uses a random number of dots tapped by a pencil onto a sheet of paper. The clustering of the dots is the significant factor. Clusters of dots indicate a positive response in that place on the paper. Tapping can be used to dowse obscured maps or graphs.

target: The target is the thing you are scrying. There are various kinds of targets. A verifiable target is a target with information that can be verified at present or in the future; it is also known as a tangible target. An occult target is a type of esoteric target related to occult symbols. An esoteric target is a non-tangible target or a target with a nonphysical basis. A mystery target is a partially tangible or non-tangible target. A symbolic target is an esoteric target involving symbols.

target pool: A collection of tasking statements for different targets that is placed into the grab bag.

tasking statement: See *statement of intent.*

team-predictive: The prediction rate when working with a team of scryers.

trance: An altered state of consciousness that is usually accompanied by a reduction in conscious mental activity.

verifiable information: Information gained from scrying (such as names, places, dates, and events) that can be verified by existing factual data.

zero-point energy: The theory that energy can arise from empty space spontaneously, and that it may be possible one day to harness that energy.

RECOMMENDED READING

Concentration: A Guide to Mental Mastery by Mouni Sadhu (London: Unwin Paperbacks, 1977).

This book contains excellent exercises for sharpening and strengthening the focus of the mind. Even though the mental state used to scry is mainly receptive, building up your mind's ability to concentrate will enable you to sustain your focus during extended mirror or crystal scryings.

Crystal Gazing and Clairvoyance by John Melville (New York: Samuel Weiser, 1970).

This reprinting of Melville's classic 1896 work is a good overview of the traditional methods used for crystal gazing during the eighteenth and nineteenth centuries. Read this to gain perspective on historical scrying rather than using it as a practical guide. In general terms, the method in this book consisted of compelling yourself to see visions in the crystal. Scryers using this method could not help but fall into the traps of anticipation bias and storytelling.

By the way, the book *Crystal-Gazing and Spiritual Clairvoyance* by L. W. de Laurence (Chicago, IL: De Laurence, Scott & Co., 1916) is a direct and complete plagiarization of Melville's book, which de Laurence, with characteristic dishonesty, published as his own work.

Crystal Vision Through Crystal Gazing by Frater Achad, the occult name of Charles Stansfeld Jones (Chicago, IL: Yogi Publication Society, 1923).

An intelligent overview by an intelligent man of the traditional method of crystal gazing. Achad was a student of Aleister Crowley.

Jacob's Rod: A Translation From the French of a Rare and Curious Work, A.D. 1693, on the Art of Findings Springs, Mines, and Minerals by Means of the Hazel Rod by J. N., translated by Thomas Welton (London: published by the translator, n.d., c. 1870).

A good text on traditional dowsing practices. You should know this background even if you do not use the traditional techniques. It is in part a translation from a French work on this subject from 1693.

John Dee's Five Books of Mystery, edited by Joseph H. Peterson (Boston, MA: Weiser Books, 2003).

This is the other half of the Enochian communications scryed by Edward Kelley and recorded by Dr. John Dee. It is a natural companion to Casaubon's *True & Faithful Relation*. The Enochian scryings of Dee and Kelley are the most extraordinary series of scryings that have ever been recorded and merit close study by all students of this ancient art.

Manual of Psychometry: The Dawn of a New Civilization by Joseph R. Buchanan (Boston, MA: published by the author, 1885).

This is a seminal text on psychometry, and it played a part in the development of my system of scrying. Well worth reading.

The Prophecies of Paracelsus: Magic Figures and Prognostications Made by Theophrastus Paracelsus About Four Hundred Years Ago, translated by J. K. (London: William Rider & Son, 1915).

This slender book is worth studying for the way in which Paracelsus worded his enigmatic prophecies. Compare the prophecies of Paracelsus with those of Nostradamus.

A True & Faithful Relation of What Passed for Many Years Between Dr. John Dee ... and Some Spirits, edited by Meric Casaubon (London: printed by D. Maxwell for T. Garthwait, 1659).

This is essential reading if you wish to understand the quality of material that can be scryed by a skilled scryer such as Edward Kelley using the traditional method of crystal gazing. Kelley's readings suffered from expectation bias and belief bias, but their complexity and scope are truly astonishing.

The Vision and the Voice by Aleister Crowley, edited by Israel Regardie (Dallas, TX: Sangreal Foundation, 1972).

This is the record of Aleister Crowley's attempt to scry the angels of the thirty Enochian Aethyrs, or Airs—thirty spirit dimensions that nest one inside the other, like Russian nesting dolls. Both Crowley's technique and the results he achieved are worthy of study.

BIBLIOGRAPHY

Abano, Peter de. *Heptameron, or Magical Elements*. In *Henry Cornelius Agrippa: His Fourth Book of Occult Philosophy*. London: Askin Publishers, 1978.

Agrippa von Nettesheim, Heinrich Cornelius. *Henry Cornelius Agrippa: His Fourth Book of Occult Philosophy*. Translated into English by Robert Turner. 1655. Facsimile edition. Contains *Of Geomancy, Magical Elements of Peter de Abano, Astronomical Geomancy, The Nature of Spirits,* and *Arbatel of Magick*. Reprint, London: Askin Publishers, 1978.

Albano, Frankie. *Miniature Albano-Waite Tarot Deck*. Stamford, CT: U.S. Games Systems, 1989.

Atkinson, William Walker. *Practical Psychomancy and Crystal Gazing*. Chicago, IL: Yogi Publication Society, 1908.

Barker, Edward B. B. *The Mendal: A Mode of Oriental Divination*. London: J. Burns, 1874.

Barrett, Francis. *The Magus, or Celestial Intelligencer; Being a Complete System of Occult Philosophy*. 1801. Facsimile, limited edition. Reprint, New York: Samuel Weiser, n.d.

Besant, Annie, and Charles W. Leadbeater. *Occult Chemistry*. London: Theosophical Publishing House, 1919.

Buchanan, Joseph R. *Manual of Psychometry: The Dawn of a New Civilization*. Boston, MA: published by the author, 1885.

Casaubon, Meric. *A True & Faithful Relation of What Passed for Many Years Between Dr. John Dee ... and Some Spirits.* London: printed by D. Maxwell for T. Garthwait, 1659.

Cayce, Edgar. *The Edgar Cayce Companion: A Comprehensive Treatise of the Edgar Cayce Readings.* Compiled by B. Ernest Frejer. New York: Barnes & Noble Digital, 2002.

———. *Edgar Cayce on Atlantis.* Edited by Hugh Lynn Cayce. New York: Paperback Library, 1968.

Crowley, Aleister. *The Thoth Tarot.* Illustrated by Lady Frieda Harris. New York: U.S. Games Systems, 1969.

———. *The Vision and the Voice.* Originally published in the periodical *The Equinox*, vol. 1, no. 5 (March 1911). Reprint, Dallas: Sangreal Foundation, 1972.

De Laurence, L. W. *Crystal-Gazing and Spiritual Clairvoyance.* Chicago, IL: De Laurence, Scott & Co., 1916.

Denton, William, and Elizabeth M. F. Denton. *Nature's Secrets; or, Psycho-metric Researches.* London: Houlston and Wright, 1863.

Dowson, Godfrey. *The Hermetic Tarot.* New York: U.S. Games Systems, 1980.

Ellis, Arthur J. *The Divining Rod: A History of Water Witching.* Washington, DC: Government Printing Office, 1917.

Grumbine, J. C. F. *Clairvoyance: The System of Philosophy Concerning the Divinity of Clairvoyance.* 3rd ed. Boston, MA: Order of the White Rose, 1904.

Hammond, D. Corydon, ed. *Handbook of Hypnotic Suggestions and Metaphors.* New York: Norton, 1990.

Hartmann, Franz. *The Principles of Astrological Geomancy: The Art of Divining by Punctuation, According to Cornelius Agrippa and Others.* London: Theosophical Publishing Co., 1889.

Melville, John. *Crystal Gazing and Clairvoyance.* 1896. Reprint, New York: Samuel Weiser, 1970.

Nicolas, Jean. *La verge de Jacob, ou l'Art de trouver les tresors, les sources, les limites, les métaux, les mines, les minéraux, et autres choses cachées, par l'usage du bâton fourché.* Lyon: Chez Hilaire Baritel, 1693.

Nostradamus. *The True Prophecies or Prognostications of Michael Nostradamus.* Translated by Theophilus de Garencières. London: Thomas Ratcliffe and Nathaniel Thompson, 1672.

Ostrander, Sheila, and Lynn Schroeder. *Psychic Discoveries Behind the Iron Curtain.* Englewood Cliffs, NJ: Prentice-Hall, 1970.

Panchadasa, Swami [William Walker Atkinson]. *A Course of Advanced Lessons in Clairvoyance and Occult Powers.* Chicago, IL: Advanced Thought Publishing Co., 1916.

Paracelsus, Theophrastus. *The Prophecies of Paracelsus: Magic Figures and Prognostications Made by Theophrastus Paracelsus About Four Hundred Years Ago.* Translated by J. K. London: William Rider & Son, 1915.

Persinger, M. A., W. G. Roll, S. G. Tiller, S. A. Koren, and C. M. Cook. "Remote Viewing with the Artist Ingo Swann: Neuropsychological Profile, Electroencephalographic Correlates, Magnetic Resonance Imaging (MRI), and Possible Mechanisms." *Perceptual and Motor Skills* 94, no. 3 (June 1, 2002): 927–49.

Peterson, Joseph H., ed. *John Dee's Five Books of Mystery: Original Sourcebook of Enochian Magic.* Boston, MA : Weiser Books, 2003.

Regardie, Israel. *A Garden of Pomegranates.* St. Paul, MN: Llewellyn, 1970.

———. *The Golden Dawn: A Complete Course in Practical Ceremonial Magic.* 1938–40. 6th ed. Four volumes in one. St. Paul, MN: Llewellyn, 1989.

Stearn, Jess. *Edgar Cayce: The Sleeping Prophet.* Garden City, NY: Doubleday, 1967.

Swann, Ingo. *Natural ESP.* New York: Bantam, 1985.

———. *Penetration: The Question of Extraterrestrial and Human Telepathy.* Rapid City, SD: Ingo Swann Books, 1998.

Thomas, Northcote W. *Crystal Gazing: Its History and Practice, with a Discussion of the Evidence for Telepathic Scrying.* London: Alexander Moring Ltd., 1905.

Trithemius, Johannes. *Steganographia: hoc est: ars per occultam scripturam animi sui voluntatem absentibus aperiendi certa…* Frankfurt, Germany: 1608.

Tyson, Jenny. *Spiritual Alchemy: Scrying, Spirit Communication, and Alchemical Wisdom.* Woodbury MN: Llewellyn, 2016.

Welton, Thomas, trans. *Jacob's Rod: A Translation From the French of a Rare and Curious Work, A.D. 1693, on the Art of Findings Springs, Mines, and Minerals by Means of the Hazel Rod.* London: published by the translator, n.d., c. 1870. The author of this French work is not, as is so often erroneously stated, Hilaire Baritel, but someone who identifies himself only as J. N.

INDEX

C

G

Garden of Pomegranates, A (Regardie), 189

Garencières, Theophilus de, 96

geomancy, 6, 115, 116

Gettysburg, 23, 29–31

Giger, Hans Ruedi, 129

glass, 13, 116, 141–144, 158, 162

gold, 52, 91, 107, 112, 143

Golden Dawn, 187, 189

Golden Dawn, The (Regardie), 189

Google Earth, 83

GPS, 82, 83, 91

grab bag, 4, 5, 9–11, 22, 27, 28, 33–38, 41, 49, 51, 63, 64, 72, 76,
    91–93, 95–99, 102, 103, 108, 119–123, 131, 132, 134, 135,
    147, 152, 154, 155, 162, 163, 177, 178, 181, 182, 186, 187,
    191, 195–197, 216, 219, 220

graphs, 60, 61, 66, 67, 69, 75, 76, 79, 86–90, 220

gray area, 64, 78, 92, 216, 217

Great Pyramid, 34, 35, 122

Great Sphinx, 28, 31, 32, 162–166

Great Table, 179–181

grid, 83, 182

grimoires, 153, 188

grounded, 19, 22, 57, 72, 73, 169, 183, 185–187, 192, 196, 204,
    216

grounding, 36

H

Hebrew, 107, 183, 188

Heptameron (Peter de Abano), 153

herbs, 117, 202, 206, 219

Hermetic Tarot, the (Dowson), 130

hieroglyphic, 182

homunculus, 152

P

Paracelsus, 222

paranormal, 5, 25, 65

patterns, 2, 17, 39, 80, 115–122, 128, 171–175, 213–215

pendulum, 3, 4, 60–63, 66–69, 77–81, 84, 86, 88–90, 97, 169, 214, 215

Penetration (Swann), 194

perceptions, 15, 16, 23, 24, 27, 32, 35, 42–45, 50, 52–56, 61, 65, 75, 81, 87, 99, 100, 103–105, 108–110, 125, 134, 135, 137, 149, 151, 153, 174, 178, 195, 198, 206, 210, 214, 216

perspective, 48, 49, 51, 104, 214

Peterson, Joseph H., 135, 222

photograph, 12, 15, 24, 76

photos, 19, 22, 24, 27, 31, 32, 56, 169, 176–179, 181, 186, 188, 205

pin, 79, 80, 84, 85, 90, 173

planets, 24, 29, 198, 215

points, 12, 13, 15–18, 40–42, 44, 47–49, 51, 52, 66, 67, 69, 72, 93, 100, 103, 110, 118–123, 128, 130–134, 136, 146, 147, 153, 155, 158, 161–163, 174, 176, 181, 184, 187, 191, 192, 196, 197, 199, 200, 214, 218

pool of targets/target pool, 6, 10, 22, 27, 31, 51, 107, 181, 182, 191, 196, 213, 214, 216, 220

practice, xiv, 5, 6, 10, 17, 18, 21, 25, 40–42, 44, 55, 57, 59, 61, 67–71, 86, 92, 100, 115, 121, 127, 129, 140, 150, 151, 154, 167–169, 179, 181, 182, 184, 189–191, 195, 196, 199–203, 207, 209, 215, 217, 219

precognition, 1, 21, 59, 199

prediction, 23, 26, 28, 53, 66, 81, 86, 89, 127, 131, 161, 169–172, 174, 175, 177–179, 205, 217, 220

predictions, 26, 59, 77, 89, 131, 168–170, 172, 173, 176, 179, 199, 200, 205, 210, 219

To Write to the Author

If you wish to contact the author or would like more information about this book, please write to the author in care of Llewellyn Worldwide Ltd. and we will forward your request. Both the author and the publisher appreciate hearing from you and learning of your enjoyment of this book and how it has helped you. Llewellyn Worldwide Ltd. cannot guarantee that every letter written to the author can be answered, but all will be forwarded. Please write to:

Jenny Tyson
℅ Llewellyn Worldwide
2143 Wooddale Drive
Woodbury, MN 55125-2989

Please enclose a self-addressed stamped envelope for reply,
or $1.00 to cover costs. If outside the U.S.A., enclose
an international postal reply coupon.

Many of Llewellyn's authors have websites with additional
information and resources. For more information,
please visit our website at http://www.llewellyn.com.

Notes

Notes

Notes

Notes

Notes